The Great Wall of Flavor

1500 Days of Chinese Recipes for Every Occasion To Whet Your Appetite, A Chinese cookbook

Chloe Lee

Editor: AALIYAH LYONS

Interior Design: BROOKE WHITE

Cover Art: DANIELLE REES

Food stylist: SIENNA ADAMS

Table Of Contents

Introduction

In the vast tapestry of global cuisines, few traditions captivate the senses and unite diverse palates with the same allure as Chinese cuisine. Steeped in a rich history that spans thousands of years, Chinese food is an art form that transcends sustenance; it's a celebration of flavors, textures, and the communal joy of sharing a meal. In this culinary voyage through the heart of China's gastronomic treasures, we embark on a journey that not only explores the intricacies of the cuisine but also pays homage to the cultural mosaic that has shaped and influenced it.

China, with its vast landscapes and distinct regional identities, boasts a culinary panorama as diverse as its people. From the fiery spices of Sichuan to the delicate nuances of Cantonese cuisine, each region contributes a unique brushstroke to the masterpiece that is Chinese food. At the core of this cookbook lies a dedication to uncovering the hidden gems of this culinary kaleidoscope, illuminating the stories behind the dishes and the people who have lovingly crafted them for generations.

within these pages, you'll find a symphony of flavors that dance across your taste buds – from the umami-rich depths of slow-cooked broths to the vibrant and crisp textures of stir-fried delights. Chinese cuisine is a harmonious blend of contrasts, balancing the sweet and the savory, the spicy and the mild, the crunchy and the tender. As we delve into these recipes, we invite you to explore not just the ingredients but the cultural narratives that infuse each dish with its distinctive character.

Our culinary expedition commences with a collection of tantalizing appetizers, each offering a sneak peek into the diverse array of flavors awaiting you. Picture yourself savoring the crisp perfection of scallion pancakes, their savory aroma wafting through the air, or the delicate balance of flavors in the iconic potsticker, each bite a testament to the skilled hands that shaped it. These appetizers, rooted in tradition, serve as a gateway to the myriad culinary wonders that follow.

Venturing further, we uncover the secrets of hearty soups that warm the soul and nourish the body. From the complex interplay of hot and sour in a steaming bowl to the comforting embrace of wonton soup, these recipes transport you to the heart of Chinese kitchens, where the alchemy of broth and aromatics transforms humble ingredients into culinary masterpieces. In each simmering pot, you'll find a reflection of the culinary wisdom passed down through generations.

No exploration of Chinese cuisine would be complete without a foray into the world of dim sum – those delightful, bite-sized creations that beckon from bamboo steamers. From the delicate folds of har gow to the comforting embrace of char siu bao, dim sum embodies the spirit of sharing and togetherness that defines Chinese dining. Our journey through these small, but mighty, dishes is a celebration of the craftsmanship and tradition that elevates dim sum to an art form.

As we reach the sweet conclusion of our culinary sojourn, we present a selection of desserts that showcase the sublime balance of flavors in Chinese sweets. Indulge in the velvety richness of egg tarts or savor the comforting warmth of red bean soup, each dessert a sweet note that lingers on the palate, leaving a lasting impression of the diverse and intricate world of Chinese cuisine.

In presenting this cookbook, our goal is not only to share recipes but to invite you into the heart of Chinese kitchens, where culinary traditions are preserved and innovation is celebrated. The beauty of Chinese cuisine lies not only in its ability to satiate hunger but in its power to tell stories, connect communities, and create cherished memories around the dining table. So, with chopsticks in hand and an open heart, let us embark on this culinary odyssey together, embracing the rich tapestry of Chinese flavors and the cultural heritage that defines them.

Chapter 1

Unraveling the Tapestry of Chinese Cuisine

Prelude to Chinese Culinary Odyssey

China, with its vast and varied landscapes, is a tapestry woven with the threads of history, culture, and culinary artistry. As we embark on this culinary odyssey, we are drawn into the allure of Chinese cuisine, a world where flavors are not merely sensations but narratives that tell the story of a civilization's journey through time.

• Unveiling the Mystique
At the heart of Chinese culinary mystique lies a deep respect for tradition coupled with an innate creativity that allows for continuous evolution. Each dish is a testament to a culinary legacy that spans thousands of years, where ancient recipes have been passed down through generations like cherished heirlooms. Unveiling this mystique involves peeling back the layers of flavors to expose the intricate techniques, the symbolism of ingredients, and the cultural nuances that make each dish unique.

Chinese cuisine embraces the philosophy that food is not merely fuel for the body but an expression of art and emotion. From the precision of knife skills to the finesse of wok tossing, every culinary act is a dance of craftsmanship and tradition. The mystique lies not just in what appears on the plate but in the centuries-old wisdom that informs the entire culinary process.

• Culinary Tapestry of China
To understand the allure of Chinese cuisine, one must appreciate the vastness and diversity that define the nation's culinary landscape. China is a country of contrast, with each region contributing its own distinct flavors, ingredients, and techniques. From the fiery kitchens of Sichuan to the delicate dim sum creations of Guangdong, the culinary tapestry of China is woven with threads of regional identity.

The northern regions boast hearty dishes rich in wheat-based staples, while the south favors the subtlety of rice and seafood. In the east, the culinary repertoire is shaped by the bounty of the sea, while the west celebrates the robust flavors of its mountainous terrain. This regional diversity is a source of pride and inspiration, making Chinese cuisine a dynamic and ever-evolving celebration of the nation's geographical and cultural abundance.

The culinary tapestry extends beyond the kitchen, integrating into every facet of Chinese life. Meals are not merely a routine but a shared experience that binds families and communities. From grand banquets during festive occasions to humble home-cooked meals, the culinary tapestry of China is interwoven with the fabric of daily life.

A Glimpse into Culinary Heritage

HISTORICAL ROOTS
MILLENNIA OF GASTRONOMIC EVOLUTION

The roots of Chinese culinary heritage run deep, intertwining with the very fabric of the nation's history. A culinary journey through China is, in essence, a voyage through millennia of gastronomic evolution. It traces its origins to ancient agricultural practices, where the cultivation of rice and wheat laid the foundation for a diverse and bountiful culinary tradition.

Chinese gastronomy's evolution can be likened to a grand tapestry woven across dynasties and epochs. Millennia ago, Chinese cooks began experimenting with various ingredients, spices, and cooking techniques, giving rise to the rich tapestry of flavors we savor today. The concept of harmony, central to Chinese philosophy, is mirrored in the culinary realm — a harmonious balance of flavors, textures, and colors that has been refined over generations.

The Silk Road, an ancient network of trade routes, played a pivotal role in introducing new ingredients and culinary techniques to China. The exchange of goods and ideas along this historic route infused Chinese cuisine with exotic spices, fruits, and cooking methods, enriching its already diverse repertoire.

CULINARY SIGNIFICANCE IN CHINESE CULTURE

Beyond sustenance, Chinese cuisine carries profound cultural significance. Meals are not mere refueling stops but communal gatherings that reflect familial bonds, respect for tradition, and an appreciation for the artistry of food. Every dish becomes a canvas for expressing cultural values, and dining is a shared experience that fosters connection and unity.

The Chinese concept of "liang wei" (两味), meaning the dual nature of flavor, underscores the importance of balancing tastes. This principle extends beyond the kitchen, symbolizing the delicate equilibrium sought in all aspects of life. Chinese culinary traditions are thus interwoven with philosophical beliefs, creating a holistic approach to nourishment that goes beyond the physical act of eating.

REGIONAL DIVERSITY
DISTINCT FLAVORS OF NORTH, SOUTH, EAST, AND WEST

China's vast expanse and diverse geography give rise to a culinary landscape that varies dramatically from one region to another. The distinct flavors of the north, characterized by hearty wheat-based dishes, stand in stark contrast to the subtlety of southern cuisine, which relies on rice and an abundance of seafood.

In the east, the coastal provinces boast a bounty of fresh seafood, influencing their culinary offerings. Meanwhile, the west, with its rugged mountains and plateaus, celebrates robust and hearty flavors. Each region's culinary identity is a reflection of its unique geography, climate, and available ingredients.

CULINARY TRADITIONS SHAPED BY GEOGRAPHY

Geography is not merely a backdrop; it's a guiding force that shapes culinary traditions. The fertile plains of the Yangtze River Delta give rise to Jiangsu and Zhejiang cuisines, known for their delicate flavors and emphasis on freshness. In contrast, the spicy and bold flavors of Sichuan cuisine find their roots in the region's mountainous terrain.

The nomadic history of the northern plains has influenced a cuisine rich in lamb and wheat-based staples. Cantonese cuisine, thriving in the Pearl River Delta's subtropical climate, showcases an array of flavors and textures, often highlighting the natural sweetness of ingredients.

In essence, regional diversity in Chinese cuisine is a testament to the adaptability and resourcefulness of its people. Ingredients unique to each region, coupled with distinct preparation methods, contribute to the kaleidoscope of flavors that defines Chinese gastronomy.

The Art of Chinese Cooking

MASTERING TECHNIQUES STIR-FRYING, STEAMING, AND SIMMERING

Chinese culinary artistry is a testament to the precision and skill embedded in its cooking techniques. At the heart of this mastery lie the three pillars of Chinese culinary techniques: stir-frying, steaming, and simmering. These methods are not just practical approaches to cooking; they are intricate dance moves in the ballet of flavors, each contributing to the harmonious symphony that defines Chinese cuisine.

STIR-FRYING

Stir-frying is the quick and dynamic technique that epitomizes the essence of Chinese cooking. The wok, a versatile and indispensable tool, takes center stage in this culinary performance. The intense heat and the concave shape of the wok allow for rapid and even cooking, with ingredients tossed and turned in a choreographed motion. This method not only preserves the natural colors, textures, and nutrients of the ingredients but also imparts the signature wok hei, or "breath of the wok," a smoky depth that elevates the overall flavor profile.

Key to successful stir-frying is the "holy trinity" of Chinese cooking: garlic, ginger, and green onions. These aromatic ingredients, along with a judicious selection of soy sauce, oyster sauce, or other seasonings, infuse stir-fried dishes with a complexity that transcends simplicity. From the sizzle of kung pao chicken to the rapid toss of vegetables in a wok, stir-frying is a technique that demands agility, timing, and an intimate understanding of ingredient textures.

STEAMING

Steaming is a gentle yet effective technique that captures the pure essence of ingredients. Chinese steaming baskets, crafted from bamboo or metal, are employed to delicately cook an array of dishes, from dumplings to whole fish. This method is favored for its ability to preserve the natural flavors and nutritional integrity of ingredients.

The art of steaming extends beyond merely placing ingredients in a steaming basket. It involves meticulous timing and an understanding of the varying textures of different foods. Dim sum classics like har gow and delicate custard-filled buns showcase the finesse required to achieve perfectly steamed morsels. The technique highlights the Chinese culinary philosophy of letting ingredients speak for themselves, with minimal interference from additional fats or oils.

SIMMERING

Simmering is the slow and patient technique that transforms humble ingredients into rich, flavorful stews and broths. This method is synonymous with nourishing comfort, as evidenced in quintessential dishes like hot and sour soup or red-braised pork. The art of simmering lies in coaxing out the depth of flavors from ingredients over extended periods, allowing them to meld and harmonize.

The selection of aromatic spices and herbs, such as star anise, cinnamon, and Sichuan peppercorns, is pivotal in creating complex and aromatic broths. Simmering not only tenderizes tougher cuts of meat but also allows the infusion of flavors to create a dish that is greater than the sum of its parts. It is a technique that demands patience, attention, and a keen sense of flavor development.

THE ARTISTRY OF KNIFE SKILLS

Knife skills in Chinese cooking are akin to a painter's brushstrokes, defining the visual and textural elements of a dish. The precision and finesse with which ingredients are sliced, diced, or julienned contribute not only to the aesthetics but also to the overall cooking process.

Chinese chefs distinguish themselves through a variety of knife techniques, each serving a specific purpose in the culinary repertoire. The julienne cut, often seen in dishes like moo shu pork, requires a deft hand to produce uniformly thin strips. Meanwhile, the precision of the chiffonade cut is showcased in dishes where delicate herbs like cilantro or basil are scattered as a finishing touch.

The cleaver, a multifunctional tool, is central to Chinese knife skills. Contrary to its Western counterpart, the Chinese cleaver is used for a myriad of tasks, from chopping bones to finely mincing garlic. The rocking motion of the cleaver, guided by the skilled hands of a chef, allows for a seamless transition between tasks, creating an efficient and fluid cooking process.

In Chinese culinary tradition, the artistry of knife skills extends beyond mere utility; it is a form of self-expression. The way in which ingredients are prepared reflects not only technical prowess but also a profound respect for the craft. It is a dance between the chef and the blade, where each cut tells a story and contributes to the symphony of flavors that define Chinese cuisine.

In the art of Chinese cooking, mastering techniques goes beyond rote execution; it requires an understanding of the philosophy that underlies each method. Stir-frying, steaming, and simmering, coupled with the artistry of knife skills, form the foundation of a culinary tradition that celebrates precision, balance, and the transformative power of heat. As we explore these techniques, we uncover the essence of Chinese culinary artistry — a marriage of skill, tradition, and an unwavering commitment to the craft.

Chapter 2

The Basics and Sauces

Grandma's Secret Hot Sauce

Prep time: 15 minutes | Cook time: 25 minutes | Makes about ¾ cup (180 ml)

- ¼ cup (60 ml) soy sauce
- ¼ cup (60 ml) sriracha
- ¼ cup (50 g) sugar

1. Combine all the ingredients in a small bowl and whisk together until the sugar is dissolved.

Basic Chinese Chicken Stock

Prep time: 5 minutes | Cook time: 3 to 4 hours |Serves 8 to 13

- 1 whole chicken
- 2 large carrots, peeled and quartered
- 1 large yellow onion, peeled and halved
- 3 scallions
- 2-inch piece ginger, peeled
- 10 to 15 cups water

1. Put the chicken, carrots, onion, scallions, and ginger in a very large pot.
2. Fill the pot with just enough water to cover the chicken.
3. Simmer on low heat for 3 to 4 hours, partially uncovered. Use an ultra-fine mesh skimmer to remove any froth from the surface, along with any excess oil.
4. Allow the stock to cool slightly then remove the solid ingredients.
5. Run the stock through a fine mesh strainer as you pour it into storage jars or containers. You can refrigerate the stock overnight then simply scoop off the solidified fat. The stock will keep in the refrigerator for up to 1 week and in the freezer for up to 6 months.

Mock Meat Dipping Sauce

Prep time: 5 minutes | Cook time: 1 minutes | Serves 4

- 2 tablespoons finely chopped fresh cilantro
- 1 tablespoon finely minced fresh ginger
- Pinch five-spice powder
- 2 tablespoons canola oil
- 2 tablespoons Chinese light soy sauce
- ½ teaspoon granulated sugar

1. In a small heatproof bowl, combine the cilantro, ginger, and five-spice powder.
2. In a skillet or a wok, heat the oil over high heat until it begins to smoke. Immediately pour the hot oil onto the ginger and cilantro. The sizzling oil will release the aroma from the herbs and spices.
3. Add the soy sauce and sugar to the bowl. Stir to combine with a spoon. Serve fresh.

Soy and Vinegar Dipping Sauce

Prep time: 3 minutes | Cook time: none | Serves 1

- 3 tablespoons soy sauce
- 2 tablespoons Chinese black vinegar
- 1 teaspoon sesame oil

1. Whisk all the ingredients together in a small bowl.

Scallion-Ginger Oil

Prep time: 5 minutes | Cook time: 5 minutes | Serves 4

- 1½ cups thinly sliced scallions
- 1 tablespoon peeled and finely minced fresh ginger
- 1 teaspoon kosher salt
- 1 cup vegetable oil

1. In a heatproof glass or stainless-steel bowl, toss the scallions, ginger, and salt. Set aside.
2. Pour the oil into a wok and heat over medium-high heat, until a piece of scallion green immediately sizzles when dropped in the oil. Once the oil is hot, remove the wok from the heat and carefully pour the hot oil over the scallions and ginger. The mixture should sizzle as you pour and bubble up. Pour the oil slowly so it does not bubble over.
3. Allow the mixture to cool completely, about 20 minutes. Stir, transfer to an airtight jar, and refrigerate for up to 2 weeks.

Orange Sauce

Prep time: 5 minutes | Cook time: 10 minutes | Serves 2/3

- 6 tablespoons orange juice
- 1 tablespoon fresh orange zest
- 2 tablespoons water
- 1 tablespoon rice vinegar
- 1 tablespoon dark soy sauce
- 2 teaspoons light soy sauce
- 2 teaspoons brown sugar
- ¼ teaspoon red pepper flakes

1. Combine the orange juice, zest, water, rice vinegar, dark soy sauce, light soy sauce, brown sugar, and red pepper flakes in a bowl.
2. Either use immediately in a stir-fry

recipe or store in a sealed container in the refrigerator until ready to use. (Use the sauce within 3 or 4 days.)

Spicy Chili Dip

Prep time: 5 minutes | Cook time: none | Serves 1

- 4 tablespoons soy sauce
- 1 to 2 teaspoons
- Chinese chili sauce
- ½ teaspoon sesame oil

1. Whisk the ingredients together in a small bowl.

All-Purpose Stir-Fry Sauce

Prep time: 5 minutes |Cook time: 5 minutes| Serves 1

- ¼ cup low-sodium soy sauce
- ¼ cup oyster sauce
- 2 tablespoons shaoxing wine
- 2 tablespoons honey or brown sugar
- 2 tablespoons water
- 1½ tablespoons sesame oil
- 1 tablespoon cornstarch
- 1 teaspoon chicken stock granules
- pinch ground white pepper

1. Pour all the ingredients into a small jar or sealable container.
2. Shake until well combined.
3. Store in the refrigerator for up to 2 weeks.

Clear Vegetable Broth

Prep time: 10 minutes | Cook time: 20 minutes | Serves 4

- 4 cups vegetable broth
- 1 cup sliced shiitake mushrooms
- 1 cup julienned carrots
- 1 cup baby bok choy, chopped
- 2 tablespoons soy sauce
- 1 tablespoon rice vinegar
- 1 teaspoon sesame oil

1. In a pot, bring vegetable broth to a simmer.
2. Add mushrooms, carrots, and bok choy to the pot. Cook until vegetables are tender.
3. Stir in soy sauce, rice vinegar, and sesame oil. Simmer for an additional 5 minutes.
4. Strain the broth before serving, discarding the solids. Serve hot.

Ginger Miso Dressing

Prep time: 6 minutes | Cook time: 10 minutes | Serves 1/2

- 1 tablespoon low-sodium soy sauce
- 1 tablespoon miso paste
- 1/4 cup rice wine vinegar
- 1/2 tablespoon sugar
- 1 teaspoon sesame oil
- 1 tablespoon toasted sesame seeds
- 1 tablespoon minced ginger
- 1 teaspoon minced garlic
- 1/4 teaspoon black pepper
- 1/4 cup vegetable or canola oil

1. In a blender, combine all the items with the exception of the vegetable oil. Pulse several times until the ingredients have broken down.
2. On the lowest setting, slowly stream in the vegetable oil and blend until dressing is fully emulsified. Dressing can be stored in the refrigerator for up to 2 days.

Chinese Chicken Soup Stock

Prep time: 15 minutes | Cook time: 25 minutes | Makes 1 gallon (3.8 l)

- 1 whole chicken, cut into 8 pieces (skin off)
- 1 lb (450 g) pork neck bones
- 4 qt (3.8 l) cold water
- 2″ (5-cm) piece ginger
- 1 clove garlic, pounded
- 2 scallions, chopped into thirds
- ½ tsp white peppercorns
- 2 tbsp (30 ml) oyster sauce
- salt to taste

1. Bring 3 quarts (2.9 L) water to a boil in a large stockpot. Add the chicken pieces and pork neck bones, and boil for about 3 to 5 minutes. This will bring out blood and scum. Pour off the water and rinse the chicken.
2. Place the chicken and pork back into the pot. Add 4 quarts (3.8 L) of cold water and all the ingredients except salt. Bring the water to a boil and cover it. Reduce the heat to a medium simmer and leave the lid slightly cracked. Simmer it for about 2 to 4 hours, skimming the scum occasionally. Season with salt to taste.
3. Let the stock cool, then strain out and discard the solids. Stock can be refrigerated for up to 4 or 5 days.

Tamarind Chili Sauce

Prep time: 5 minutes | Cook time: 15 minutes | Serves ¼

- 3 tablespoons tamarind juice concentrate
- 1½ tablespoons fish sauce
- 1 tablespoon warm water
- ½ tablespoon lime juice
- 1 tablespoon palm sugar
- 1 teaspoon minced garlic
- 1 red chili, minced finely

1. In a medium bowl, whisk together all the ingredients and refrigerate for 15 minutes.
2. Sauce can be stored in the refrigerator for up to 1 week.

Hoisin Peanut Dipping Sauce

Prep time: 15 minutes | Cook time: 25 minutes | Makes about 1 cup (240 ml)

- ½ cup (120 ml) hoisin sauce
- 3 tbsp (45 ml) creamy peanut butter
- ¼ cup (60 ml) water
- 1 tbsp (15 ml) rice vinegar

1. Prepare the sauce by combining all the ingredients until thoroughly mixed.

Spicy Garlic Sauce for Stir-Fry

Prep time: 10 minutes | Cook time: 5 minutes | Serves 4

- 3 tablespoons soy sauce
- 2 tablespoons rice vinegar
- 1 tablespoon sesame oil
- 2 teaspoons sugar
- 1 tablespoon finely minced garlic
- 1 teaspoon chili flakes (adjust to taste)
- 2 tablespoons vegetable oil

1. In a bowl, mix soy sauce, rice vinegar, sesame oil, and sugar until sugar dissolves.
2. In a small pan, heat vegetable oil over medium heat. Add minced garlic and chili flakes. Cook until garlic is golden but not browned.
3. Pour the hot oil mixture into the sauce bowl. Stir well and use immediately for stir-frying.

Vegan Cashew Sauce

Prep time: 5 minutes | Cook time: 5 minutes | Serves 10

- 1 cup hot water
- 1 ½ cups raw cashews
- 2 garlic cloves
- ¼ cup nutritional yeast
- ½ teaspoon ground cumin
- ½ teaspoon onion powder
- Toppings:
- ½ small tomato, chopped
- ¼ cup green bell pepper, finely chopped
- 3 tablespoons cilantro, chopped
- ½ cup vegan chorizo

1. Roast cashews in a Mandarin wok for 5 minutes until golden-brown.
2. Transfer the cashews to a food processor.
3. Add rest of the queso ingredients to the food processor and blend until smooth.
4. Serve.

Szechuan Peanut Sauce

Prep time: 8 minutes | Cook time: 5 minutes | Serves 4

- 1/2 cup peanut butter
- 3 tablespoons soy sauce
- 2 tablespoons rice vinegar
- 1 tablespoon sesame oil
- 1 tablespoon Szechuan peppercorns, crushed
- 1 teaspoon sugar
- 1 clove garlic, minced

1. In a saucepan over low heat, combine peanut butter, soy sauce, rice vinegar, sesame oil, crushed Szechuan peppercorns, sugar, and minced garlic.
2. Stir until the mixture is smooth and heated through. Adjust consistency with water if needed.
3. Let it cool before serving. Excellent for dipping or drizzling over noodles.

Sweet and Sour Sauce

Prep time: 5 minutes |Cook time: 5 minutes| Serves 1

- 5 tablespoons ketchup
- 3 tablespoons water
- 1½ tablespoons apple cider vinegar
- 1 tablespoon plum sauce
- 1 tablespoon cornstarch
- 2 teaspoons soy sauce
- 2 teaspoons brown sugar

1. Combine all the ingredients in a small bowl.
2. Stir well to combine, using the back of the spoon to break up any cornstarch clumps, until the cornstarch has completely dissolved.

Chinese Hot Pot Broth

Prep time: 15 minutes | Cook time: 30 minutes | Serves 4

- 6 cups vegetable or chicken broth
- 3 slices ginger
- 2 cloves garlic, crushed
- 2 tablespoons soy sauce
- 1 tablespoon sesame oil

1. In a pot, combine broth, ginger, garlic, soy sauce, sesame oil, green onions, star anise, and cinnamon stick.
2. Bring to a boil, then simmer for 20-30 minutes to infuse flavors.
3. Strain the broth before serving in a hot pot. Adjust seasoning as needed. Enjoy with a variety of ingredients for dipping.

Bloody Mary Dipping Sauce

Prep time: 5 minutes | Cook time: 30 minutes | Serves 1½

- 1 (14½-ounce) can diced tomatoes, drained
- 2 tablespoons tomato paste or ketchup
- 1 teaspoon Tabasco sauce
- ½ teaspoon celery salt
- ¼ teaspoon ground pepper

1. Place all the ingredients into a large bowl. Using an immersion blender, pulse until the ingredients have incorporated and the texture of the sauce is somewhat smooth.
2. This can also be done in a blender. Refrigerate for 30 minutes before serving. Sauce can be stored in the refrigerator for up to 2 days.

Plum Sauce

Prep time: 15 minutes | Cook time: 1 hour | Serves 2

- 4 cups coarsely chopped plums (about 1½ pounds)
- ½ small yellow onion, chopped
- ½-inch fresh ginger slice, peeled
- 1 garlic clove, peeled and smashed
- ½ cup water
- ⅓ cup light brown sugar
- ¼ cup apple cider vinegar
- ½ teaspoon Chinese five spice powder
- Kosher salt

1. In a wok, bring the plums, onion, ginger, garlic, and water to a boil over medium-high heat. Cover, reduce the heat to medium, and simmer, stirring occasionally, until the plums and onion are tender, about 20 minutes.
2. Transfer the mixture to a blender or food processor and blend until smooth. Return to the wok and stir in the sugar, vinegar, five spice powder, and a pinch of salt.
3. Turn the heat back to medium-high and bring to a boil, stirring frequently. Reduce the heat to low and simmer until the mixture reaches the consistency of applesauce, about 30 minutes.
4. Transfer to a clean jar and cool to room temperature. Refrigerate for up to a week or freeze for up to a month.

Pickled Vegetables

Prep time: 30 minutes | Cook time: 5 minutes | Serves 4

- 1/2 seedless cucumber and 1/2 large-headed cauliflower, cut into broad florets
- 225 g carrots (4 medium-sized) cut into sticks
- 3 tablespoons of coarsely chopped garlic and ginger
- 1 tablespoon mustard seeds (preferably black or brown)
- 1 teaspoon of coriander seeds and ground turmeric
- 1/2 teaspoon of cumin seeds and 1/2 teaspoon of fennel seeds
- 1/3 cup vegetable oil and 5 dried hot red chilies,
- 1/2 cup of distilled white vinegar
- 3 tablespoons wrapped dark brown sugar
- Equipment
- an electric coffee / spice grinder;
- a well seasoned 35 cm flat-bottom wok

1. Preheat the oven to 120 ° C, with the grid in the middle, cut off the end of the cucumber and then cut it in half lengthways. Boil the cauliflower and carrots together in a large saucepan with salted boiling water (1 1/2 tablespoons of salt for 3 liters of water), stirring occasionally for 1 minute.
2. Drain in a colander then place the colander in an ice bath. Arrange the cauliflower, carrots and cucumbers in a layer in a 43 x 30 cm flat baking pan and bake, stirring occasionally, until the vegetables are dry and slightly limp (approx. 30 minutes).
3. Pulse garlic and ginger with a teaspoon of salt in a food processor for 30 minutes until finely ground, then place in a bowl. Woke over high heat until a drop of water evaporates immediately.
4. Add the vegetables, vinegar and brown sugar and bring to the boil while stirring until the sugar has dissolved. Transfer to a shallow bowl and allow to cool to room temperature, stirring occasionally, approx. 1 hour; Transfer to an airtight container and allow to cool, shake once or twice a day for 1 week (so that the aromas can develop).

Chapter 3

Poultry

Tangerine Peel Chicken

Prep time: 5 minutes | Cook time: 25 minutes | Serves 4

- 4 tangerines or 2 oranges (preferably organic) with peels, cut into quarters
- 1 tablespoon peeled and chopped fresh ginger
- 5 garlic cloves, peeled
- ¾ cup coconut sugar
- ¾ cup chicken broth
- ½ cup plum sauce, hoisin sauce, or korean bbq sauce
- 1½ teaspoons sriracha
- 1 teaspoon raw apple cider vinegar
- ¼ teaspoon five-spice powder
- 2 tablespoons extra-virgin olive oil
- 8 boneless, skinless chicken thighs
- sea salt
- ground black pepper

1. Preheat your broiler.
2. Combine the tangerines, ginger, garlic, sugar, broth, plum sauce, sriracha, vinegar, and five-spice powder in a blender. Blend until the mixture is really smooth. Set aside.
3. Heat the oil in a large sauté pan over medium-high heat.
4. Season the chicken generously with salt and pepper. Add the chicken to the pan. Cook until it is brown on one side, about 5 minutes. Flip and brown the other side, about 5 minutes more.
5. When the chicken is browned, pour enough of the tangerine sauce into the pan so that the chicken is mostly covered. Stir to coat the chicken.
6. Cover the pan and cook until the chicken is cooked through, about 15 minutes.
7. Using tongs, remove the chicken from the pan, shaking off any excess sauce, and transfer it to a rimmed baking sheet.
8. Broil until the chicken just starts to char, about 3 minutes. Serve and enjoy!

Five-Spice Roast Duck

Prep time: 15 minutes | Cook time: 2 hours | Serves 4

- 1 whole duck (about 4-5 pounds)
- 2 tablespoons Chinese five-spice powder
- 2 teaspoons salt
- 1 tablespoon honey
- 2 tablespoons soy sauce
- 2 tablespoons Shaoxing wine
- 3 slices ginger
- 3 green onions, cut into 2-inch pieces

1. Preheat the oven to 350°F (175°C).
2. Rub the duck inside and out with five-spice powder and salt.
3. Mix honey, soy sauce, and Shaoxing wine. Brush the mixture over the duck.
4. Place ginger and green onions inside the duck cavity.
5. Roast in the oven for about 2 hours, basting with the pan juices every 30 minutes, until the skin is crispy and the duck is cooked through.

Tea-Smoked Duck Breast

Prep time: 10 minutes | Cook time: 15 minutes | Serves 4

- 4 boneless, skin-on duck breasts
- 1 teaspoon fine sea salt
- 2 tablespoons loose jasmine tea
- ¼ cup uncooked long-grain white rice
- ¼ cup brown sugar
- 2 tablespoons all-purpose flour
- plum sauce, for dipping

1. Lightly score the duck skin with perpendicular cuts ¼-inch apart, making sure not to cut down into the meat.
2. Place the breasts skin-side down in the wok and heat on medium-high until the fat begins to render and sizzle. Then reduce the heat to medium and cook for 5 minutes.
3. Drain the fat from the wok. Turn the duck breast over and cook for another 5 minutes.
4. Remove the duck breasts, drain the fat, and wipe out the wok.
5. Combine the tea leaves, rice, brown sugar, and flour on a square piece of aluminum foil and roll the edges up to form the foil into a shallow, ½-inch-deep saucer. The top should be open. Place the foil saucer in the bottom of the wok.
6. Place a rack inside the wok and put the duck breasts on the rack. Cover the wok with a domed lid.
7. If you're cooking indoors, open any windows near the stove and turn your exhaust fan on high. If you don't have a way to exhaust air outside, do the next steps outdoors.
8. Turn the heat on high. As the mixture heats, it will begin to smoke. At first, the smoke will be white, then light yellow, then darker yellow. When it turns dark yellow (after about 5 minutes), turn the heat to low.
9. For a light smoke, set a timer for 3 minutes. For heavier smoke, smoke the breasts for 5 to 10 minutes longer.
10. Remove and slice the breasts into ½-inch pieces across the grain and serve with plum sauce.

Delicious Chicken Wings

Prep time: 25 minutes | Cook time: 40 minutes | Serves 4

- 900 gr. chicken wings
- 1/2 cup of chicken broth with reduced sodium content
- 2 teaspoons of soy sauce
- 2 teaspoons of cornstarch
- 1 teaspoon of sugar
- 2 tablespoons of peanut or vegetable oil
- 1 tablespoon of fermented black beans from china (drained)
- 1 tablespoon of finely chopped garlic
- 2 teaspoons of finely chopped peeled fresh ginger
- 1/8 teaspoon dried hot red pepper flakes
- a well-seasoned 35 cm flat-bottom wok with a lid

1. Pat the chicken wings dry, cut off the tips with a large, heavy knife and throw them away and cut the wings in half at the joint. Mix the broth, soy sauce, cornstarch and sugar in a small bowl until the sugar is dissolved.
2. Woke over high heat until a bead of water evaporates immediately. Pour in oil and swirl around the wok to brush. Add the chicken wings and a pinch of salt and stir-fry, allowing the wings to rest for 5 to 10 seconds between stirs, until golden brown, 8 to 10 minutes.

Chicken, Carrots & Snow Peas Stir Fry

Prep time: 5 minutes | Cook time: 5 minutes | Serves 2

- 1/2 pound chicken
  1 cup carrots
- 1 cup snow peas
- 1 tsp. oil

1. Marinade chicken in a Superfoods marinade. Stir fry drained chicken in coconut oil for few minutes, add all vegetables and stir fry for 2 more minutes.
2. Add the rest of the marinade and stir fry for a minute. Serve with brown rice or quinoa.

Peruvian Chicken with Green Sauce

Prep time: 10 minutes | Cook time: 1 hour | Serves 4

For The Chicken:
- 3 garlic cloves, minced
- 1 tablespoon extra-virgin olive oil
- 1 tablespoon ground cumin
- 1 tablespoon paprika
- ½ teaspoon dried oregano
- grated zest of 1 lemon
- juice of 1½ lemons
- 1 (4½-pound) chicken (preferably organic) spatchcocked (backbone removed and pressed flat—your butcher can do this for you)
- ½ teaspoon sea salt

For The Green Sauce:
- 1 bunch fresh cilantro, thick stems discarded
- 1 (1-inch) piece serrano pepper (or to taste)
- 1 garlic clove, chopped
- juice of 1½ limes
- pinch sea salt
- ⅓ cup mayonnaise (i like to use an avocado oil–based mayo)

1. Preheat the oven to 400°F.
2. Combine the garlic, olive oil, cumin, paprika, oregano, lemon zest, and lemon juice in a small bowl.
3. Lay the chicken, skin-side up, on a rimmed baking sheet. Gently loosen the skin from the breast and the thighs by slipping two fingers between the skin and the flesh. Spread about 2 tablespoons of the spice mixture under the chicken skin, spreading it as evenly as you can. Season the outside of the chicken with the salt.
4. Roast the chicken, brushing it with the remaining spice mixture every 20 minutes, until an instant-read thermometer inserted in the thigh registers 170°F, about 1 hour.
5. Transfer the chicken to a cutting board and let it rest for 10 to 15 minutes.
6. Meanwhile, to make the sauce, combine all the sauce ingredients in a blender and blend until smooth.
7. Carve the chicken and serve it with the sauce on the side. Enjoy!

Chicken Lettuce Wraps

Prep time: 9 minutes | Cook time: 40 minutes | Serves 4

- 2 tablespoons oyster sauce
- 1 tablespoon soy sauce
- 1 tablespoon rice wine vinegar
- 1 teaspoon sesame oil
- 1 teaspoon sugar
- 1/2 teaspoon black pepper
- 1/2 pound boneless, skinless chicken breast, sliced into thin strips
- 4 tablespoons vegetable oil, divided
- 1/2 tablespoon minced garlic
- 2 shallots, thinly sliced
- 1 cup sliced oyster mushrooms
- 1/2 cup shiitake mushrooms
- 1/4 cup chicken broth
- 2 scallions, cut into 1″ pieces
- 8 Bibb lettuce leaves
- 1/2 cup Peking Sauce

1. In a medium bowl, whisk together the oyster sauce, soy sauce, rice wine vinegar, sesame oil, sugar, and black pepper. Add the chicken and toss to coat. Refrigerate for 30 minutes.
2. Heat a wok over medium heat, then add 2 tablespoons oil. Add the garlic and shallots and cook for 30 seconds, then add the mushrooms. Toss the items in the wok several times and then pour in the chicken broth. Cook the mushrooms until tender, about 4–5 minutes. Remove to a plate.
3. Add the remaining oil to the wok; once it is heated, add in the chicken. Stir-fry for 2–3 minutes.
4. Add the mushroom mixture back into the wok along with the scallions. Cook together for another 2 minutes.
5. To assemble the wraps, divide the mixture into eighths. Take 1 lettuce leaf and place 1 portion of the chicken mixture in the center. Serve with Peking Sauce as a dipping condiment.

Baby Corn, Snow Peas & Chicken Stir Fry

Prep time: 5 minutes | Cook time: 5 minutes | Serves 2

- 1/2 pound chicken 1 cup baby corn
- 1/2 cup snow peas
- 1/2 cup julienned carrot
- 1/2 cup sliced mushrooms
- 1/2 cup sliced red peppers
- 1 tbsp. coconut oil

1. Marinade shrimp in a Superfoods marinade. Stir fry drained chicken in coconut oil for few minutes, add all vegetables and stir fry for 2 more minutes.
2. Add the rest of the marinade and stir fry for a minute. Serve with brown rice or quinoa.

Crispy Chicken and Red Chiles

Prep time: 20 minutes | Cook time: 20 minutes | Serves 4

For The Chicken:
- 2 pounds chicken, cut into 1-inch pieces
- 3 tablespoons shaoxing cooking wine or dry sherry
- 3 tablespoons dark soy sauce
- 1 cup potato starch
- 1 tablespoon freshly ground sichuan peppercorns
- 1 tablespoon ground red chili powder or cayenne pepper
- 2 teaspoons sea salt
- cooking oil, for deep-frying

For The Sauce:
- 10 garlic cloves, sliced
- 1 teaspoon freshly ground sichuan peppercorns
- 3 tablespoons doubanjiang (chinese chili bean paste)
- 2 tablespoons minced fresh ginger
- 1 cup dried red chiles
- ¼ teaspoon sea salt

To Make The Chicken:
1. In a large bowl, combine the chicken, wine, and soy sauce, toss to coat, and let sit to marinate while you prepare the rest of the dish.
2. In a small, shallow bowl, combine the potato starch, ground Sichuan peppercorns, chili powder, and salt.
3. Remove the chicken from the marinade a few pieces at a time (shaking off excess marinade), dredge in the spiced starch mixture, and put on a plate.
4. In the wok, heat 2 inches of oil over high heat until it shimmers. Fry the chicken, turning occasionally, for about 10 minutes, until golden.

5. Deep-fry the chicken in two to three batches, allowing enough room for the chicken to cook on all sides. Once cooked, transfer the chicken to a paper towel–lined plate. Once all the chicken is fried, transfer the remaining oil to a heatproof jar or bowl. Return 3 tablespoons of oil to the wok.

To Make The Sauce:
1. In the wok, heat the oil on high heat until it shimmers.
2. Add the garlic and stir-fry until fragrant, about 10 seconds. Add the ground Sichuan peppercorns, doubanjiang, and ginger, and stir-fry until the sauce becomes a red-orange color.
3. Return the chicken pieces to the wok and toss to coat with the sauce. Add the dried red chiles and salt, and stir-fry for 2 minutes. Serve hot.

Lemon Chicken

Prep time: 15 minutes | Cook time: 20 minutes | Serves 4

- 4 boneless, skinless chicken breasts
- Salt and pepper to taste
- 1 cup flour
- 2 eggs, beaten
- 1/4 cup vegetable oil
- 1/2 cup chicken broth
- 1/4 cup honey
- 1/4 cup soy sauce
- Zest and juice of 2 lemons
- 2 tablespoons cornstarch (optional for thickening)
- Sesame seeds and sliced green onions for garnish

1. Season chicken breasts with salt and pepper. Dredge in flour, dip in beaten eggs, and fry in vegetable oil until golden brown and cooked through.
2. In a saucepan, combine chicken broth, honey, soy sauce, lemon zest, and lemon juice. Bring to a simmer.
3. If desired, mix cornstarch with a little water to create a slurry. Add to the sauce to thicken.
4. Pour the lemon sauce over the fried chicken. Garnish with sesame seeds and sliced green onions before serving.

Pineapple Chicken

Prep time: 15 minutes | Cook time: 30 minutes | Serves 4

- 3 tablespoons of soy sauce
- 3 tablespoons of olive oil, divided
- 1/2 teaspoon paprika
- salt to taste
- 1 pound boneless and skinless chicken breast (cut into strips)
- 1 red pepper (diced)
- 1 bunch of spring onions (cut into 5 cm pieces)
- 1 can of pineapple chunks (drained and retained juice)
- 1 tablespoon of cornstarch

1. Mix salt, soy sauce, paprika and 2 tablespoons of olive oil in a bowl. Turn the chicken strips in it. Let it marinate while the remaining ingredients are cooked.
2. Heat the remaining 1 tablespoon of olive oil in a wok. Fry the peppers for 3 minutes while stirring; add the spring onions. Fry and stir for another 2 minutes. Remove the chicken from the marinade and place in the wok; Drain the marinade.
3. Cook for 10-15 minutes, stirring occasionally, until the chicken is completely cooked and no longer pink in the middle.
4. Mix cornstarch and pineapple juice in a bowl. Put the pineapple pieces in the pan and cook for 2-3 minutes.
5. Add the pineapple juice mixture and bring to the boil. Let it simmer for 3 minutes, until the sauce is thick.

Sesame Chicken and Shiitake Stir-Fry

Prep time: 30 minutes | Cook time: 20 minutes | Serves 4

- 2 pounds boneless skinless chicken breasts (4 halves), cut across into 1.5 cm thick slices
- 2 tbsp water, 2 tbsp rice vinegar and 2 tbsp soy sauce
- 2 teaspoons of sugar
- 1/2 teaspoon dried hot red pepper flakes
- 3 tbsp vegetable oil and 1 large onion, halved lengthways
- 1 pound fresh shiitake mushrooms, stems removed and caps quartered
- 1 1/4 cups frozen peas (thawed)
- 2 tbsp sesame seeds (toasted)
- Side dish: steamed rice

1. Pat the chicken dry and season with salt. In a small bowl, stir together the soy sauce, vinegar, water, red pepper flakes and sugar until the sugar has dissolved. - Heat a pan or wok over high heat until a drop of water drips onto the cooking surface of the wok and evaporates immediately. Pour 1 tablespoon of oil into it, swirl the wok to distribute the oil evenly on the hob and heat the oil until it is hot and smokes slightly.

2. Add the onions and sauté for 2 minutes or until the onions are tender, crispy and golden in color. Place the sauteed onions in a large bowl. Add 1/2 tablespoon of oil to the hot wok and heat the pan until it starts to smoke and stir-fry half of the chicken for about 1 1/2 minutes or until the chicken is just about cooked through.

3. Put the cooked chicken in the bowl with the sauteed onions and fry the rest of the chicken in half a tablespoon of oil while stirring, just like you fried the first half of the chicken and then add it to the same bowl the sauteed onions and the first half of the cooked chicken.

4. Put the sesame and vinegar mixture in the wok and let it cook until it just boils, then mix in the chicken mixture and fry for about 1 minute until it is through. Season with salt and pepper and serve with rice.

Chicken, Chinese Cabbage & Mushrooms Stir Fry

Prep time: 5 minutes | Cook time: 5 minutes | Serves 2

- 1 cup sliced Chinese cabbage 1/2 pound chicken
- 1 cup sliced mushrooms
- 1/2 cup sliced green onions
- 1 tbsp. oil

1. Marinade chicken in Superfoods marinade. Stir fry drained chicken in coconut oil for few minutes, add all vegetables and stir fry for 2 more minutes.

2. Add the rest of the marinade and stir fry for a minute. Serve with brown rice or quinoa.

Creamy Apple Cider Vinegar Chicken

Prep time: 5 minutes | Cook time: 40 minutes | Serves 4

- 1⅓ pounds boneless, skinless chicken thighs (7 or 8 thighs)
- sea salt
- ground black pepper
- 1 tablespoon extra-virgin olive oil
- 1 medium onion, sliced
- 4 large garlic cloves, minced
- ⅔ cup raw apple cider vinegar
- 1 cup chicken broth
- 5 fresh thyme sprigs
- 1 (13-ounce) can full-fat coconut milk (you will use only the cream on top; save the liquid for your smoothies or another use)

1. Season the chicken with salt and pepper.
2. Heat the oil in a large skillet over medium-high heat. Add the chicken and cook, undisturbed, until brown on one side, about 5 minutes. Flip the chicken and cook until it is browned on the other side, about 5 minutes more. Transfer the browned chicken to a plate.
3. Add the onion and garlic to the pan and cook for 1 minute.
4. Pour in the vinegar to deglaze the pan, scraping up any browned bits from the bottom.
5. Pour in the broth. Return the chicken to the pan and add the thyme sprigs.
6. Cover and simmer for 10 minutes. Flip the chicken over, cover the pan again, and continue cooking until the chicken is cooked through, about 10 minutes more. Transfer the chicken to a plate.
7. Add the coconut cream to the pan and whisk it into the cooking liquid until it is fully incorporated. Simmer until the sauce thickens a bit, about 5 minutes.
8. Return the chicken to the pan and simmer until the chicken is heated through.
9. Discard the thyme sprigs. Serve and enjoy!

Chicken with Marsala Wine

Prep time: 7 minutes | Cook time: 30 minutes | Serves 4

- 1 pound boneless, skinless chicken breasts
- 6 tablespoons dry Marsala wine, divided
- ½ teaspoon salt
- ½ teaspoon black pepper
- 2 teaspoons cornstarch
- ¼ cup chicken broth
- 3½ tablespoons olive oil, divided
- 2 thin slices ginger, chopped
- 2 cloves garlic, chopped
- 2 shallots, chopped
- ¼ pound fresh mushrooms, thinly sliced
- 1 tablespoon chopped fresh basil leaves
- 1 tablespoon chopped Italian parsley, for garnish

1. Cut the chicken breasts into thin strips approximately 1½–2 long. Place the chicken strips in a bowl and add 2 tablespoons wine, salt, black pepper, and cornstarch. Marinate the chicken for 20 minutes.
2. In a small bowl, combine the chicken broth and 4 tablespoons wine. Set aside.
3. Add the broth and wine mixture. Bring to a boil, then add the chicken back into the pan. Stir in the chopped basil. Stir-fry for 2 more minutes to blend all the ingredients and make sure the chicken is cooked through. Garnish with the fresh parsley.

General Tso's Chicken

Prep time: 15 minutes | Cook time: 15 minutes | Serves 4

- 1 pound boneless, skinless chicken thighs, cut into bite-sized pieces
- 1/2 cup cornstarch
- 3 tablespoons soy sauce
- 2 tablespoons rice vinegar
- 2 tablespoons hoisin sauce
- 1 tablespoon sugar
- 1 tablespoon sesame oil
- 3 cloves garlic, minced
- 1 tablespoon fresh ginger, minced
- 1 teaspoon chili flakes (adjust to taste)
- 2 green onions, sliced
- Toss chicken pieces in cornstarch until evenly coated.

1. In a pan, heat oil over medium-high heat. Fry chicken until golden brown and crispy. Set aside.
2. In another pan, combine soy sauce, rice vinegar, hoisin sauce, sugar, and sesame oil. Add garlic, ginger, and chili flakes. Cook until fragrant.
3. Add the fried chicken to the sauce, tossing until well-coated. Garnish with sliced green onions before serving.

Chicken and Cashew Stir-Fry

Prep time: 20 minutes | Cook time: 10 minutes | Serves 4

- 1 bunch of spring onions
- 1 pound boneless skinless chicken thighs
- 1/2 teaspoon of salt
- 1/4 teaspoon black pepper
- 3 tablespoons of vegetable oil
- 1 chopped red pepper
- 4 cloves of finely chopped garlic
- 1 1/2 tablespoons of fresh ginger
- 1/4 teaspoon dried red pepper flakes

- 3/4 cup reduced sodium chicken broth
- 1 1/2 teaspoons of soy sauce
- 1 1/2 teaspoons of cornstarch
- 1 teaspoon of sugar
- 1/2 cup of salted, roasted whole cashews

1. Cut the spring onions and separate the green and white parts. Pat the chicken dry and cut it into pieces, then season with salt and pepper.
2. Heat a (non-stick) frying pan or wok over moderately high heat until water droplets form on the cooking surface of the wok. Pour in the oil, swirl the wok to distribute the oil, and stir-fry the chicken for 4-5 minutes, until just cooked through and golden brown in places.
3. Use a slotted spoon to place the fried chicken on a plate. Add red pepper flakes, spring onions, bell pepper, ginger, and garlic to the same wok and stir-fry for 5-6 minutes or until the peppers are just tender.
4. Reduce the heat and let it simmer for 1-2 minutes, stirring occasionally, or until the sauce is thick. Add the spring onions, the cooked chicken along with the juice on the plate and the cashews and mix them together.

Sweet-and-Sour Chicken

Prep time: 10 minutes | Cook time: 5 minutes | Serves 4

- 1 pound boneless, skinless chicken thighs, cut into ¼-inch pieces across the grain
- 2 tablespoons brown sugar
- 2 tablespoons shaoxing cooking wine
- 2 tablespoons rice vinegar
- 1 tablespoon light soy sauce
- ¼ cup ketchup
- 2 tablespoons cooking oil
- 1 tablespoon chopped, fresh ginger
- 2 garlic cloves, crushed and chopped
- 1 medium onion, cut into ½-inch pieces
- 1 teaspoon cornstarch
- 4 scallions, both white and green parts, cut into ¼-inch pieces
- rice or noodles, for serving

1. In a bowl, combine the sliced chicken, brown sugar, wine, vinegar, soy sauce, and ketchup.
2. In the wok, heat the oil over medium-high heat until it shimmers. Add the ginger, garlic, and chicken, reserving any liquid, and stir-fry for 2 minutes, until fragrant.
3. Add the onion and stir-fry for 1 minute. Add the bell pepper and stir-fry for 1 minute, until the onion pieces begin to separate.
4. Add the cornstarch and reserved liquid to the wok and stir-fry for about 2 minutes, until a glaze is formed, and the chicken is cooked through.
5. Add the scallions and serve over rice or noodles.

Five-Spice Chicken and Cucumber Stir-Fry

Prep time: 15 minutes | Cook time: 5 minutes | Serves 4

- 1 pound boneless, skinless chicken thighs, sliced into ¼-inch strips against the grain
- 1 tablespoon chinese five-spice powder
- 2 tablespoons shaoxing cooking wine
- 2 tablespoons light soy sauce
- 1 tablespoon brown sugar
- 1 teaspoon spicy sesame oil
- 1 tablespoon cornstarch
- 2 tablespoons cooking oil
- 1 tablespoon chopped fresh ginger
- 2 garlic cloves, crushed and chopped
- 2 cups cucumbers, skin on (run a fork along their lengths to break up the skin before slicing them into bite-size pieces)
- 4 scallions, both white and green parts, cut into ¼-inch pieces
- rice or noodles, for serving

1. In a medium bowl, combine the chicken, five-spice powder, wine, soy sauce, brown sugar, sesame oil, and cornstarch.
2. In the wok, heat the cooking oil over medium-high heat until it shimmers.
3. Add the ginger, garlic, and chicken, reserving the liquid. Stir-fry for 2 minutes, until fragrant.
4. Add the remaining liquid and the sliced cucumbers and stir-fry for 1 minute, until the chicken is cooked through, and the cucumbers are warmed.
5. Add the scallions and stir-fry for 1 minute to mix well. Serve over rice or noodles.

Crispy Duck and Pancakes

Prep time: 20 minutes | Cook time: 1 ½ to 2 hours | Serves 4

- 4 whole duck legs
- For Overnight Salting
- 1 teaspoon 5-spice powder
- 1 teaspoon Sichuan peppercorns, crushed
- 1 teaspoon salt
- For Baking
- 1 teaspoon honey
- ¾ cup chicken stock
- For Pancakes
- 2 cups flour, unsifted
- ¾ cup water
- Sesame oil
- For Serving
- Spring onions, julienned
- Cucumber sticks
- Hoisin sauce

1. Prick the duck legs all over using a fork or knife. Rub the salting ingredients into the duck legs. Let them sit, covered and refrigerated, overnight or for a few hours.
2. Preheat the oven to 400°F, and pat the duck legs dry with paper towels.
3. Place the duck legs face down in a non-stick frying pan.
4. Cook over high heat, not turning, until the skin begins to become crisp and brown (about 5 minutes). Flip them over and brown the other side as well.
5. Arrange the browned duck legs in a baking pan or oven-proof dish.
6. Drizzle them with honey and pour in the chicken stock.
7. Bake for 20 minutes, and then reduce the oven temperature to 275°F and bake for 1 hour. The duck flesh should fall off the bone at this point.
8. While the duck legs are in the oven, prepare the pancake dough. (See below)
9. When the duck legs are ready, remove them from the oven and let them cool for a short while.
10. Shred the duck meat with 2 forks, sprinkle it with spring onion, and serve it with hot pancakes, cucumber, and hoisin sauce.

To Make Pancakes

1. Boil the water.
2. Place the flour in a bowl and make a well in the center.
3. Add the hot water and mix. You may gradually add more flour to get a kneadable dough.
4. Knead the dough on a floured surface for 5 minutes, then cover and let it rest for 30 minutes.
5. Knead it again for 5 minutes, and roll it into a 1 ½-inch cylinder.
6. Divide the cylinder into 16 pieces, and roll each piece into a smooth ball.
7. Spread some sesame oil on your hands and flatten a ball of dough.
8. Roll it into a smooth disc, and brush the top with sesame oil. Make another disc of a similar size and place on top of first disc. Roll them out into a 6- to7-inch diameter double disc. Repeat for the rest of the dough balls.
9. Heat a skillet until water sprinkled into it bounces about in a small balls. Brush on a thin coat of sesame oil. Cook the double pancakes for 30 seconds on each side, without any browning. Remove them from the pan and slap them on a hard surface to separate the 2 discs. Peel away the 2 discs from each other, and place them on a sheet of foil. Repeat this procedure for the rest of the discs.
10. To steam the pancakes, form a packet by sealing foil over the discs. Place the foil packet in a steamer or double boiler and steam it for 20-30 minutes.

Chicken, Onion & Green & Red Peppers Stir Fry

Prep time: 5 minutes | Cook time: 5 minutes | Serves 2

- 1/2 pound chicken
  1/2 cup sliced onions
- 1/2 cup sliced green peppers
- 1/2 cup sliced red peppers
- 1/2 cup cashews
- 1 tsp. oil

1. Marinade chicken in a Superfoods marinade. Stir fry drained chicken in coconut oil for few minutes, add all vegetables and stir fry for 2 more minutes.
2. Add the rest of the marinade and stir fry for a minute. Serve with brown rice or quinoa.

Chicken with Bean Sprouts

Prep time: 5 minutes | Cook time: 30 minutes | Serves 4

- 1 pound boneless, skinless chicken breasts
- 1 tablespoon white rice vinegar
- 1 tablespoon soy sauce
- 2 teaspoons cornstarch
- 2 tablespoons dark soy sauce
- 2 tablespoons water
- 1 teaspoon sugar
- 3 tablespoons vegetable oil, divided
- 2 slices ginger
- 1/4 teaspoon salt
- 2 1/2 cups mung bean sprouts, trimmed

1. Cut the chicken breasts into thin strips approximately 1 1/2–2 long. Place the chicken strips in a bowl and add the white rice vinegar, soy sauce, and cornstarch. Marinate the chicken for 20 minutes.
2. In a small bowl, combine the dark soy

sauce, water, and sugar. Set aside.

3. Heat a wok or skillet on medium-high heat until it is almost smoking. Add 2 tablespoons oil. When the oil is hot, add the ginger slices. Let brown for 2–3 minutes, then remove. (This is to flavor the oil.)
4. Add the chicken strips. Let them brown briefly, then stir-fry, stirring and tossing the chicken for 3–4 minutes, until it turns white and is nearly cooked. Remove the chicken from the pan.
5. Heat 1 tablespoon oil in the wok or skillet. When the oil is hot, add the salt and the mung bean sprouts. Stir-fry for 1 minute, then add the soy sauce mixture.
6. Add the chicken back into the pan. Stir-fry for 2 more minutes to heat everything through. Serve hot.

Chinese Orange Chicken

Prep time: 5 minutes | Cook time: 30 minutes | Serves 4

- 1 large egg
- ¾ cup chickpea flour or all-purpose flour
- 1½ pounds boneless, skinless chicken thighs, cut into bite-size pieces
- sea salt
- ground black pepper
- 1 tablespoon extra-virgin olive oil
- 3 garlic cloves, chopped
- 1 tablespoon minced fresh ginger
- 1½ cups fresh orange juice
- grated zest of 1 orange
- 3 tablespoons raw honey
- 1 tablespoon coconut aminos or soy sauce
- 1 tablespoon no-sugar-added orange marmalade
- ½ teaspoon red pepper flakes
- 1½ tablespoons cornstarch whisked into 6 tablespoons water

1. Preheat the oven to 375°F. Line a rimmed baking sheet with parchment paper or aluminum foil.
2. Beat the egg in a shallow dish. Put the flour in another shallow dish.
3. Season the chicken with salt and pepper. Dredge the chicken pieces first in the egg and then in the flour.
4. Lay the coated chicken in a single layer on the baking sheet.
5. Bake until the chicken is cooked through and starting to brown, about 20 minutes.
6. In a medium pot, heat the oil over medium heat. Add the garlic and ginger and stir for 1 minute.
7. Add the orange juice and zest, honey, aminos, marmalade, and red pepper flakes and bring the mixture to a boil, stirring often. Reduce the heat and simmer until the sauce starts to thicken a bit, about 4 minutes.
8. Add the chicken to the pot and stir to coat. Enjoy!

Kung Pao Chicken

Prep time: 15 minutes | Cook time: 15 minutes | Serves 4

- 1 pound boneless, skinless chicken thighs, cut into bite-sized pieces
- 2 tablespoons soy sauce
- 1 tablespoon Shaoxing wine
- 1 tablespoon cornstarch
- 2 tablespoons vegetable oil
- 1/2 cup unsalted peanuts
- 3 dried red chili peppers
- 3 cloves garlic, minced
- 1 tablespoon fresh ginger, minced
- 2 green onions, sliced

1. In a bowl, marinate chicken with soy sauce, Shaoxing wine, and cornstarch.
2. In a wok or pan, heat oil over high heat. Stir-fry chicken until cooked through. Remove and set aside.
3. In the same pan, add peanuts and dried chili peppers. Stir-fry until fragrant.
4. Add garlic and ginger, stir-fry briefly, then add the cooked chicken back to the pan.
5. Toss everything together, garnish with sliced green onions, and serve.

Chapter 4

Beef, Pork, and Lamb

Chinese Aromatic Honey Pork

Prep time: 15 minutes | Cook time: 5 minutes | Serves 4

- 1 pound ground pork
- 1 tablespoon shaoxing cooking wine
- 1 tablespoon honey
- 1 teaspoon spicy sesame oil
- 2 tablespoons cooking oil
- 1 tablespoon chopped fresh ginger
- 2 garlic cloves, crushed and chopped
- 1 (15-ounce) can straw mushrooms, drained and rinsed
- 2 tablespoons soy sauce
- 4 scallions, both white and green parts, cut into ¼-inch pieces
- rice or noodles, for serving

1. In a bowl, combine the pork, wine, honey, and sesame oil.
2. In the wok, heat the cooking oil over high heat until it shimmers.
3. Add the ginger, garlic, and pork mixture and stir-fry for 2 minutes, until fragrant and browned.
4. Add the mushrooms and soy sauce and stir-fry for 1 minute, until well mixed.
5. Add the scallions and stir-fry for 1 minute, until well mixed.
6. Serve over rice or noodles.

Szechuan Beef Recipe

Prep time: 20 minutes | Cook time: 5 minutes | Serves 2

- 8 ounces beef tenderloin, cut into strips
- Marinade
- 1 teaspoon cornstarch
- ½ teaspoon rice wine
- 1 teaspoon dark soy sauce
- Sauce
- ½ tablespoon oyster sauce
- ½ tablespoon chili garlic sauce
- 1 ½ teaspoons soy sauce
- 2 teaspoons sugar
- 2 tablespoons water
- ½ teaspoon chili oil
- ½ teaspoon sesame oil
- Other Ingredients
- 2 tablespoons oil, divided
- 2 cloves garlic, minced
- ¼ small green bell pepper, julienned
- ¼ small red bell pepper, julienned
- 1 small carrot, julienned
- ½ teaspoon chili oil or according to taste
- 2 stalks green onion, cut into strips

1. Combine the ingredients for the marinade. Stir in the beef, and marinate for 15-30 minutes.
2. In a bowl, mix together the sauce ingredients, and set aside.
3. Heat a wok over high heat. Add 1 tablespoon of oil and sear the beef until partly browned. Transfer it to a paper-lined plate.
4. Scrape off any brown bits from the wok, and add the remaining oil.
5. Add garlic and stir-fry until fragrant.
6. Stir in the peppers and carrot. Cook for about 30 seconds, and add the beef back to the wok.
7. Pour in the sauce mixture and stir well.
8. Add the green onion and chili oil. Stir for 30 seconds, or until the sauce is of the desired thickness.
9. Serve.

Bacon-Wrapped Shrimp

Prep time: 5 minutes | Cook time: 10 minutes | Serves 6

- 24 extra-large shrimp, deveined and shelled, with tails on
- 1/2 teaspoon black pepper
- 6 slices bacon, quartered
- 1 tablespoon vegetable oil
- 2 cups Basil Pesto

1. Season shrimp with pepper. One at a time, wrap a piece of bacon around each shrimp. Use a toothpick to secure.
2. Heat oil in a wok over medium heat. Add the wrapped shrimp in a single layer. Cook for 2 minutes on each side or until the bacon is crispy and the shrimp turn pink. Drain the shrimp on plates lined with paper towels. Repeat until all the shrimp have been cooked.
3. Serve warm with pesto as a dipping sauce.

Edamame, Asparagus, Pork & Snow Peas Stir Fry

Prep time: 5 minutes | Cook time: 5 minutes | Serves 2

- 1/2 pound cubed pork
  1 cup sliced asparagus
- 1/2 cup snow peas
- 1/2 cup sliced onions
- 1/2 cup edamame
- 1 tsp. oil

1. Marinade pork in a Superfoods marinade. Stir fry drained pork in coconut oil for few minutes, add all vegetables and stir fry for 2 more minutes.
2. Add the rest of the marinade and stir fry for a minute. Serve with brown rice or quinoa.

Plain Mongolian Beef

Prep time: 15 minutes | Cook time: 5 minutes | Serves 4

- 1/4 cup soy sauce
- 1 tablespoon of hoisin sauce
- 1 tablespoon of sesame oil
- 2 teaspoons of white sugar
- 1 tablespoon of chopped garlic
- 1 tablespoon red pepper flakes (optional)
- 450 g beef flank steak, (thinly sliced)
- 1 tablespoon of peanut oil
- 2 large green onions, (thinly sliced)

1. Whisk the soy sauce, hoisin sauce, sesame oil, sugar, garlic and red pepper flakes in a bowl.
2. Pour the marinade over the beef, cover and place in the fridge for 1 hour overnight. Heat the peanut oil in a wok or in a large, non-stick pan over high heat.
3. Add the green onions and cook for 5 to 10 seconds before stirring in the beef.
4. Boil and stir until the beef is no longer pink and begins to brown, about 5 minutes.

Pork, Mushrooms & Basil Stir Fry

Prep time: 5 minutes | Cook time: 5 minutes | Serves 2

- 1/2 pound cubed pork
  1 cup sliced mushrooms
- 1/2 cup basil leaves
- 1/2 cup sliced carrots and cucumbers
- 1 tsp. oil

1. Marinade pork in a Superfoods marinade. Stir fry drained pork in coconut oil for few minutes, add all vegetables and stir fry for 2 more minutes.
2. Add the rest of the marinade and stir fry for a minute. Serve with brown rice or quinoa.

Broccoli, Yellow Peppers & Beef Stir Fry

Prep time: 5 minutes | Cook time: 5 minutes | Serves 2

- 1/2 pound beef
  1 cup broccoli
- 1/2 cup sliced yellow peppers
- 1/2 cup chopped onions
- 1 tbsp. sesame seeds
- 1 tsp. oil

1. Marinade beef in a Superfoods marinade. Stir fry drained beef in coconut oil for few minutes, add all vegetables and stir fry for 2 more minutes.
2. Add the rest of the marinade and stir fry for a minute. Serve with brown rice or quinoa.

Chinese Lamb Stir-Fry with Cumin

Prep time: 15 minutes | Cook time: 15 minutes | Serves 4

- 1 pound lamb leg or shoulder, thinly sliced
- 2 tablespoons soy sauce
- 1 tablespoon Shaoxing wine
- 1 tablespoon hoisin sauce
- 2 teaspoons ground cumin
- 1 teaspoon ground coriander
- 1 teaspoon chili powder (adjust to taste)
- 2 tablespoons vegetable oil
- 1 onion, thinly sliced
- 1 bell pepper, thinly sliced
- 3 cloves garlic, minced
- Fresh cilantro for garnish

1. In a bowl, mix soy sauce, Shaoxing wine, hoisin sauce, cumin, coriander, and chili powder. Add the sliced lamb, ensuring it's well-coated. Marinate for 10 minutes.
2. Heat vegetable oil in a wok or skillet over high heat. Stir-fry the marinated lamb until browned. Remove from the pan and set aside.
3. In the same pan, add a bit more oil if needed. Stir-fry onion and bell pepper until softened.
4. Add minced garlic and continue to stir-fry until fragrant.
5. Return the cooked lamb to the pan, toss everything together, and cook for an additional minute. Garnish with fresh cilantro before serving over rice or noodles.

Spicy Poached Beef

Prep time: 15 minutes | Cook time: 5 minutes | Serves 4

- 1 pound thin-sliced sirloin steak, cut across the grain
- 1 teaspoon spicy sesame oil
- 1 tablespoon chinese five-spice powder
- 1 tablespoon soy sauce
- 1 tablespoon shaoxing cooking wine
- 1 tablespoon oyster sauce
- ¼ cup plus 1 tablespoon cornstarch, divided
- 2 tablespoons cooking oil
- 1 tablespoon chopped fresh ginger
- 3 garlic cloves, crushed and chopped
- 2 cups gai lan (chinese broccoli), cut into 2-inch pieces
- 2 cups broth (meat, seafood, or vegetable)
- 1 (15-ounce) can straw mushrooms, drained and rinsed
- 4 scallions, both white and green parts, cut into ¼-inch pieces, for garnishing

1. In a bowl, combine the steak, sesame oil, five-spice powder, soy sauce, wine, oyster sauce, and ¼ cup of cornstarch, and mix well.
2. In the wok, heat the cooking oil over high heat until it shimmers.
3. Add the ginger, garlic, and gai lan, and stir-fry for 1 minute, until fragrant.
4. Add the broth and the mushrooms, and bring to a simmer.
5. Let the steak simmer for 2 minutes, then stir in the remaining 1 tablespoon of cornstarch to thicken slightly.
6. Garnish with the scallions and serve over rice or noodles.

Black Pepper Flank Steak

Prep time: 10 minutes | Cook time: 15 minutes | Serves 4

- 1 pound flank steak
- 4 teaspoons light soy sauce, divided
- 3 teaspoons cornstarch, divided
- 1 teaspoon sugar
- 1 tablespoon water
- 1 tablespoon oyster sauce
- 1 teaspoon freshly ground black pepper
- 2 teaspoons neutral oil, divided
- 2 red bell peppers, chopped
- ½ sweet onion, sliced
- ¼ cup beef broth or water
- Cooked rice or noodles, for serving

1. Using a sharp chef's knife, cut the flank steak with the grain into 4 strips, then cut the strips into ¼-inch-thick bite-size pieces. Transfer to a medium bowl. Stir in 3 teaspoons of soy sauce, 1 teaspoon of cornstarch, and the sugar. Set aside to marinate for 10 minutes.
2. In a small bowl, whisk the water, oyster sauce, remaining 1 teaspoon of soy sauce, remaining 2 teaspoons of cornstarch, and pepper. Set aside.
3. On the Instant Pot, select Sauté and adjust the heat to high. Pour in 1 teaspoon of oil. Once hot, add the bell peppers and stir-fry for 2 minutes until crisp-tender. Transfer the bell peppers to another medium bowl.
4. Pour the remaining 1 teaspoon of oil into the pot and add the onion. Stir-fry for about 2 minutes until soft. Add the beef, spreading it out, and stir-fry for 1 browned bits from the bottom.
5. Lock the lid. Program to pressure cook for 5 minutes on high pressure.
6. When the timer sounds, quick release the pressure.
7. Carefully remove the lid, select Sauté again, and add the bell peppers. Whisk the cornstarch slurry and stir it into the pot. Cook, stirring, for about 1 minute until the sauce bubbles and thickens. Serve immediately with rice or noodles.

Pork, Cauliflower & Chinese Celery Stir Fry

Prep time: 5 minutes | Cook time: 5 minutes | Serves 2

- 1/2 pound cubed pork
  1/2 cup chopped cauliflower
- 1/2 cup sliced broccoli
- 1/2 cup sliced red peppers
- 1/2 cup sliced Chinese celery
- 1 tsp. oil

1. Marinade pork in a Superfoods marinade. Stir fry drained pork in coconut oil for few minutes, add all vegetables and stir fry for 2 more minutes.
2. Add the rest of the marinade and stir fry for a minute. Serve with brown rice or quinoa.

Zucchini with Lamb Stir Fry

Prep time: 10 minutes | Cook time: 15 minutes | Serves 4

- 450 gr. of ground lamb
- 4 tablespoons of soy sauce
- 1 tablespoon of chopped fresh ginger
- 1 tablespoon of chopped garlic
- 2 teaspoons plus 2 tablespoons of cornstarch
- 1 cup of canned low-salt chicken stock
- 2 tablespoons of fresh lemon juice
- 2 teaspoons of garlic and chili sauce
- 3 tablespoons of vegetable oil
- 2 tablespoons of oriental sesame oil
- 3 large cloves of peeled garlic
- 600 g zucchini (cut into strips)

1. Mix the lamb, 2 tablespoons soy sauce, ginger, minced garlic and 2 teaspoons cornstarch in a large bowl. Mix the broth, lemon juice, chili sauce and the remaining 2 tablespoons of soy sauce and 2 tablespoons of cornstarch in a small bowl.
2. Heat both oils in a wok or in a Dutch oven over high heat. Add 3 cloves of garlic; Cook for about 2 minutes until golden brown.
3. Discard the garlic. Add the zucchini and onion; Fry while stirring until they are crispy and tender, about 3 minutes.
4. Add green onions. Fry, stirring, until wilted, about 1 minute. Put the vegetables on a plate. Put the lamb mixture in the wok; Fry, stirring, until the meat is brown, about 3 minutes.
5. Add the stock mixture; Cook, stirring constantly, until the sauce becomes thick, about 1 minute. Return the vegetables to the wok; Keep frying, stirring constantly, until the sauce is heated.
6. Season with salt and pepper. Serve with rice.

Chinese BBQ Pork

Prep time: 10 minutes | Marinating time: 4 hours or overnight | Cook time: 30 minutes | Serves 4

- 1 pound pork shoulder, cut into thin strips
- 2 tablespoons soy sauce
- 2 tablespoons hoisin sauce
- 2 tablespoons honey
- 1 tablespoon oyster sauce
- 1 tablespoon Shaoxing wine
- 1 teaspoon five-spice powder
- 1 teaspoon sesame oil
- 2 cloves garlic, minced
- Red food coloring (optional for traditional color)
- 1 tablespoon vegetable oil (for basting)

1. In a bowl, mix soy sauce, hoisin sauce, honey, oyster sauce, Shaoxing wine, five-spice powder, sesame oil, garlic, and food coloring if using.
2. Add the pork strips to the marinade, ensuring each piece is coated. Marinate in the refrigerator for at least 4 hours or overnight.
3. Preheat the oven to 375°F (190°C). Thread the pork strips onto skewers or lay them on a rack over a baking sheet.
4. Bake for 20 minutes, basting with vegetable oil halfway through, until the pork is cooked through and has a nice char.
5. Slice and serve the BBQ pork over rice or noodles.

Spinach and Goat Cheese-Stuffed Pork Chops

Prep time: 7 minutes | Cook time: 10 minutes | Serves 2

- 4 tablespoons vegetable oil, divided
- 1/4 cup minced shallots
- 1/2 tablespoon minced garlic
- 6 ounces frozen spinach, thawed and drained
- 5 ounces goat cheese
- 2 boneless pork chops, 1/2–3/4 thickness
- 1/2 teaspoon kosher salt
- 1/4 teaspoon black pepper
- 1 cup white wine
- 1 tablespoon unsalted butter
- 1/2 tablespoon whole grain or Dijon mustard
- 1/2 teaspoon fresh thyme leaves

1. Heat 2 tablespoons oil in a wok over medium heat. Add the shallots and garlic and cook for 30 seconds.
2. Add the spinach and stir-fry for 1 minute. Remove from heat.
3. Mix the goat cheese with the spinach mixture in a small bowl. Set aside and allow to cool to room temperature.
4. Cut a small pocket into each pork chop, being careful not to cut all the way through. Season the pork with salt and pepper. Stuff each chop with a few spoonfuls of the cooled spinach mixture. If needed, use toothpicks to help keep chop closed.
5. Wipe the inside of the wok with paper towels. Heat the remaining oil over medium heat. Add the pork chops to the wok and cook for 3–4 minutes on each side until golden brown. Remove the chops and cover loosely with foil to keep warm.
6. Add the wine to the wok and turn the heat to medium high. Scrape up the bottom of the wok to loosen the flavorful brown bits. Allow 2–3 minutes for the wine to reduce by half, then whisk in the butter, mustard, and thyme. Cook for 1 minute and then spoon the sauce over the stuffed pork chops. Serve hot.

Asparagus, Sesame Beef & Red Peppers Stir Fry

Prep time: 5 minutes | Cook time: 5 minutes | Serves 2

- 1/2 pound beef
  1 cup sliced red pepper
- 1 cup sliced carrots
- 1/2 cup sliced onions
- 1/2 sesame seeds
- 1 tsp. oil

1. Marinade beef in a Superfoods marinade. Roll drained beef in sesame seeds and stir fry in coconut oil for few minutes with asparagus.
2. Add other vegetables and stir fry for 4 more minutes.
3. Add the rest of the marinade and stir fry for a minute. Serve with brown rice or quinoa.

Miso-Glazed Pork Belly

Prep time: 7 minutes | Cook time: 10 minutes | Serves 2

- 2 tablespoons low-sodium soy sauce
- 1 tablespoon miso paste
- 1 tablespoon honey
- 1 tablespoon mirin
- 1 tablespoon water
- 1 tablespoon vegetable oil
- 1/2 pound pork belly, sliced into 1/4 pieces
- 1 cup cooked white rice
- 1 teaspoon toasted sesame seeds
- 1 scallion, green part only, diced

1. In a small bowl, whisk together the soy sauce, miso paste, honey, mirin, water, sesame oil, and garlic. Set aside.
2. Heat a wok over medium heat and add the oil. Swirl the pan and add the pork belly. Cook for 1–2 minutes on each side until both sides of the pork belly have turned golden brown and some of the fat has rendered out. You may need to use paper towels to blot out excess fat.
3. Pour the soy sauce glaze into the wok and lower the heat. Cover and simmer the pork for 6–8 minutes, flipping the pork halfway through.
4. Serve the pork belly over bowls of rice and drizzle glaze on top. Sprinkle toasted sesame seeds and scallion over the bowls and serve immediately.

Beef & Yellow Peppers Stir Fry

Prep time: 5 minutes | Cook time: 5 minutes | Serves 2

- 1/2 pound beef
  2 sliced yellow peppers
- 1 sliced red or orange pepper
- 1/2 cup sliced onions
- 1 tbsp. coconut oil
- 1/2 cup broccoli florets
- 1/2 cup mushrooms
- 1/2 cup sliced zucchini or celery or both

1. Marinade beef in a Superfoods marinade. Stir fry drained beef in coconut oil for few minutes, add all veggies and stir fry for 2 more minutes.
2. Add the rest of the marinade and stir fry for a minute. Serve with brown rice or quinoa.

Beef with Orange Peel

Prep time: 25 minutes | Cook time: 6 hours | Serves 6

- 600 gr. beef sirloin, thinly sliced
- 1 tablespoon low-sodium soy sauce
- 1 tablespoon of cornstarch
- 1 teaspoon of dark sesame oil
- 1/2 teaspoon baking powder
- 1 tablespoon low-sodium soy sauce
- 2 tablespoons of frozen orange juice concentrate, (thawed)
- 1 tablespoon rice vinegar
- 1 teaspoon of dark sesame oil
- 1 tablespoon of brown sugar
- 1 teaspoon corn starch
- 1 tablespoon of peanut oil
- 3 cloves of garlic, (chopped)
- 1 tablespoon of chopped fresh ginger root
- 1 tablespoon of finely grated orange peel
- 1/4 teaspoon red pepper flakes

1. Mix the beef, 1 tablespoon soy sauce, 1 tablespoon cornstarch, 1 teaspoon sesame oil and baking soda in a bowl and mix everything well. Heat peanut oil in a wok or large non-stick pan over high heat and refrigerate for 1 to 3 hours.
2. Stir in garlic, ginger, orange peel and red pepper flakes and cook for 20 to 30 seconds until the garlic begins to brown.
3. Add the beef; cook and stir until the beef starts to turn brown and crispy, about 5 minutes.
4. Whisk 1 tablespoon of soy sauce, orange juice concentrate, rice vinegar, 1 teaspoon of sesame oil, brown sugar and 1 teaspoon of cornstarch in a small bowl.
5. Stir into the beef and cook until the sauce has thickened and turned clear, about 30 seconds.

Pork Liver, Green Beans & Zucchini Stir Fry

Prep time: 5 minutes | Cook time: 5 minutes | Serves 2

- 1/2 pound cubed pork liver
  1 cup sliced green beans
- 1/2 cup sliced zucchini
- 1/2 cup sliced celery and few red chili peppers
- 1 tsp. oil

1. Marinade liver in a Superfoods marinade. Stir fry drained liver in coconut oil for few minutes, add all vegetables and stir fry for 2 more minutes.
2. Add the rest of the marinade and stir fry for a minute. Serve with brown rice or quinoa.

Steamed Minced Pork with Egg

Prep time: 30 minutes | Cook time: 10 minutes | Serves 4

- 1 pound boneless country-style pork ribs or pork butt
- 2 teaspoons light soy sauce
- 1 teaspoon sugar
- 1 teaspoon cornstarch
- 1 large egg, lightly beaten
- 1 cup water, plus 1 tablespoon, divided

1. Use a cleaver or chef's knife to dice the pork. Then, chop from left to right, fold the meat over, rotate it 90 degrees, and repeat until the pork is a fine mince. Transfer to a medium bowl. Stir in the soy sauce, sugar, and cornstarch. Add the egg and mix until combined. Transfer the pork to a pressure-safe bowl and smooth it down so it cooks evenly. Add 1 tablespoon of water to the bowl.
2. Pour the remaining 1 cup of water into the Instant Pot and place a trivet inside. Place the bowl of pork meat on the trivet.
3. Lock the lid. Program to pressure cook for 10 minutes on high pressure.
4. When the timer sounds, let the pressure release naturally for 5 minutes, then quick release the remaining pressure.

Beef Stir-Fry with Vegetables

Prep time: 5 minutes | Cook time: 20 minutes | Serves 4

- ¾ pound boneless sirloin
- Oyster-Flavored Marinade for Beef
- 3 tablespoons vegetable or peanut oil, divided
- 2 thin slices ginger
- 1 teaspoon salt
- ½ cup canned sliced bamboo shoots, rinsed
- 1 tablespoon Chinese rice wine, dry sherry, or water
- 1 medium zucchini, cut on the diagonal into ½ slices
- 1 medium red bell pepper, seeded and cut into strips lengthwise
- ½ teaspoon black pepper

1. Cut the beef across the grain into thin strips approximately 2 long. Place the beef in a bowl and add the marinade. Marinate the beef for 15 minutes.
2. Heat a wok or skillet on medium-high heat until it is nearly smoking. Add 2 tablespoons oil, swirling the wok or skillet so that it covers the sides. When the oil is hot, add the ginger and let brown for 2–3 minutes. Remove the pieces of ginger.
3. Add the beef, laying it flat in the pan. Let sear for about 30 seconds, then stir-fry the beef, moving it around quickly with a spatula until the beef is no longer pink and is nearly cooked through. Remove and drain in a colander or on paper towels.
4. Clean out the wok and add 1 tablespoon oil. When the oil is hot, add salt and the bamboo shoots. Stir-fry briefly for about 1 minute, splashing the bamboo shoots with the rice wine or sherry.
5. Add the zucchini and bell pepper. Continue stir-frying for about 2 minutes or until the zucchini turns a darker color and is tender but still firm.
6. Add the beef back into the skillet and season with black pepper. Stir-fry for another minute to mix all the ingredients together. Serve immediately.

Beef, Onions & Chili Stir Fry

Prep time: 5 minutes | Cook time: 5 minutes | Serves 2

- 1/2 pound beef
  1 cup sliced onions
- 1/2 cup sliced celery
- 1 tbsp. coconut oil
- 1 tsp. chili sauce (to taste)

1. Marinade pork in a Superfoods marinade with chili sauce added. Stir fry drained beef in coconut oil for few minutes, add onions and celery and stir fry for 2 more minutes.
2. Add the rest of the marinade and red peppers and stir fry for a minute. Serve with brown rice or quinoa.

Black Bean Beef with Asparagus

Prep time: 5 minutes | Cook time: 23 minutes | Serves 3

- 1 pound flank or sirloin steak
- 1/4 cup Oyster-Flavored Marinade for Beef
- 3 1/2 tablespoons vegetable or peanut oil, divided
- 1/2 teaspoon minced ginger, divided
- 1/2 teaspoon minced garlic, divided
- 2 tablespoons Chinese black bean sauce
- 1/2 pound asparagus, cut on the diagonal into thin slices
- 1/4 cup chicken broth
- 1 teaspoon granulated sugar

1. Cut the steak across the grain into thin strips 1 1/2–2 long. Place the beef strips in a bowl and add the marinade. Marinate the beef for 15 minutes.
2. Heat a wok or skillet over medium-high heat until it is nearly smoking and add 2 tablespoons oil. When the oil is hot, add half the ginger and garlic. Stir-fry for 10 seconds.
3. Add half the beef. Stir-fry the beef for 2 minutes or until it is no longer pink and is nearly cooked. Remove and drain in a colander or on paper towels. Stir-fry the remainder of the beef.
4. Heat 1 1/2 tablespoons oil in the wok or skillet. When the oil is hot, add the remainder of the garlic and ginger. Stir-fry for 10 seconds.
5. Add the black bean sauce. Stir-fry for about 15 seconds, mixing with the garlic and ginger.
6. Add the asparagus to the wok or skillet. Stir-fry for 1 minute, then add the chicken broth and bring to a boil. Cover and cook until the asparagus turns a bright green and is tender but still crisp (about 2 more minutes).
7. Uncover and add the beef back into the pan. Stir in the sugar. Stir-fry for 1–2 more minutes to mix everything together. Serve hot.

Chapter 5

Fish and Seafood

Roasted Lemon Shrimp and Scallions

Prep time: 5 minutes | Cook time: 8 minutes | Serves 4

- 1¼ pounds large raw shrimp, peeled and deveined, tails left on
- 1 tablespoon extra-virgin olive oil
- ½ teaspoon dried oregano
- 2 large lemons, 1 zested and juiced, 1 thinly sliced
- sea salt
- ground black pepper
- 1 (4-ounce) bunch scallions with roots, cut into 1-inch pieces

1. Preheat the oven to 400°F. Line a rimmed baking sheet with parchment paper or aluminum foil.
2. Put the shrimp on the baking sheet. Add the oil, oregano, lemon zest, and lemon juice; season with salt and pepper to taste. Toss to combine well and spread the shrimp in a single layer.
3. Scatter the scallion pieces and lemon slices all around the shrimp.
4. Roast until the shrimp are almost done but not cooked completely through, about 5 minutes.
5. Remove the baking sheet from the oven and change the setting to broil.
6. Broil for 2 minutes or until the shrimp are cooked through and the lemon slices just start to darken.
7. Discard the scallion roots. Serve and enjoy!

Fried Shrimps with Garlic and White Pepper

Prep time: 5 minutes | Cook time: 5 minutes | Serves 4

- 8 cloves of garlic, minced, or more to taste
- 2 tablespoons of tapioca flour
- 2 tablespoons of fish sauce
- 2 tablespoons of light soy sauce
- 1 tablespoon of white sugar
- 1/2 teaspoon of ground white pepper
- 1/4 cup vegetable oil, divided or as needed
- 450 gr. whole unpeeled prawns (divided)

1. Mix the garlic, tapioca flour, fish sauce, soy sauce, sugar and white pepper in a bowl, add the prawns and place in the coat.
2. Heat 2 tablespoons of oil in a heavy pan over high heat. Add 1/2 of the prawns in a single layer; Fry until golden brown and crispy, 1 to 2 minutes per side.
3. Repeat with the remaining oil and the remaining shrimp.

Mussels in Saffron Sauce

Prep time: 6 minutes | Cook time: 10 minutes | Serves 4

- 2 tablespoons olive oil
- 2 tablespoons unsalted butter
- 1 large shallot, thinly sliced
- 3 large garlic cloves, finely minced
- 1 cup dry white wine
- ½ cup clam juice or chicken stock
- ¼ teaspoon saffron threads
- 3 pounds black mussels, scrubbed and debearded
- 1½ teaspoons kosher salt
- 1 teaspoon ground black pepper
- ¼ cup flat-leaf parsley, chopped

1. Heat a wok or large skillet over medium heat and add the olive oil and butter. Once the oil is hot and butter has melted, add in the shallots and garlic and stir-fry for 30 seconds.
2. Season with salt and pepper. Transfer contents to a large serving dish and sprinkle the top with the parsley. Serve immediately.

Whole Steamed Fish with Sizzling Ginger

Prep time: 10 minutes | Cook time: 20 minutes | Serves 4

For The Fish:
- 1 whole whitefish, about 2 pounds, head on and cleaned
- ½ cup kosher salt, for cleaning
- 3 scallions, both white and green parts, sliced into 3-inch pieces
- 4 peeled, fresh ginger slices, each about the size of a quarter
- 2 tablespoons shaoxing cooking wine

For The Sauce:
- 2 tablespoons light soy sauce
- 1 tablespoon sesame oil
- 2 teaspoons sugar

For The Sizzling Ginger Oil:
- 3 tablespoons cooking oil
- 2 tablespoons peeled fresh ginger, finely julienned into thin strips, divided
- 2 scallions, both white and green parts, thinly sliced, divided
- red onion, thinly sliced (optional)
- chopped fresh cilantro (optional)

To Make The Fish:
1. Rub the fish inside and out with the kosher salt. Rinse the fish and pat dry with paper towels.
2. On a plate large enough to fit into a bamboo steamer basket, make a bed using half of each of the scallions and ginger. Lay the fish on top and stuff the remaining scallions and ginger inside the fish. Pour the wine over the fish.
3. Rinse a bamboo steamer basket and its lid under cold water and place it in the wok. Pour in about 2 inches of cold water, or until it is above the bottom rim of the steamer by about ¼ to ½ inch, but not so high that the water touches the bottom of the basket. Bring the water to a boil.
4. Place the plate in the steamer basket and cover. Steam the fish over medium heat for 15 minutes (add 2 minutes for every half pound more). Before removing from the wok, poke the fish with a fork near the head. If the flesh flakes, it's done. If the flesh still sticks together, steam for 2 minutes more.

To Make The Sauce:
1. While the fish is steaming, in a small pan, warm the soy sauce, sesame oil, and sugar over low heat. Set aside.
2. Once the fish is cooked, transfer to a clean platter. Discard the cooking liquid and aromatics from the steaming plate. Pour the warm soy sauce mixture over the fish. Tent with foil to keep it warm while you prepare the oil.

To Make The Sizzling Ginger Oil:
1. In a small saucepan, heat the cooking oil over medium heat. Just before it starts to smoke, add half of each of the ginger and scallions and fry for 10 seconds. Pour the hot, sizzling oil over the top of the fish.
2. Garnish with the remaining ginger, scallions, red onion (if using), and cilantro (if using) and serve immediately.

Chinese-Style Steamed Fish

Prep time: 10 minutes | Cook time: 15 minutes | Serves 4

- 1 whole fish (such as sea bass or snapper), scaled and gutted
- 3 tablespoons soy sauce
- 2 tablespoons rice vinegar
- 1 tablespoon sesame oil
- 1 tablespoon sugar
- 3 slices ginger
- 2 green onions, sliced
- Fresh cilantro for garnish

1. Score the fish on both sides. Place on a heatproof dish.
2. Mix soy sauce, rice vinegar, sesame oil, and sugar. Pour over the fish.
3. Place ginger slices on top and inside the fish cavity.
4. Steam the fish for 15 minutes or until cooked through.
5. Garnish with sliced green onions and fresh cilantro before serving.

Squid, Green Peppers & Red Peppers Stir Fry

Prep time: 5 minutes | Cook time: 5 minutes | Serves 2

- 1 cup sliced green peppers
  1/2 pound squid
- 1 cup sliced red peppers
- 1/2 cup sliced onions
- 1 tbsp. oil

1. Marinade squid in Superfoods marinade. Stir fry drained squid in coconut oil for few minutes, add all vegetables and stir fry for 2 more minutes.
2. Add the rest of the marinade and stir fry for a minute. Serve with brown rice or quinoa.

Cantonese-Style Lobster

Prep time: 20 minutes | Cook time: 15 minutes | Serves 2

- 2 lobster tails, split in half
- 2 tablespoons soy sauce
- 1 tablespoon oyster sauce
- 1 tablespoon Shaoxing wine
- 1 tablespoon sugar
- 2 tablespoons vegetable oil
- 3 cloves garlic, minced
- 1 teaspoon ginger, minced
- 2 green onions, sliced

1. Preheat the oven broiler. Place lobster tails on a baking sheet.
2. Mix soy sauce, oyster sauce, Shaoxing wine, and sugar. Brush over the lobster tails.
3. Broil for 10-15 minutes or until the lobster is cooked and slightly charred.
4. In a pan, heat vegetable oil. Sauté minced garlic and ginger until fragrant.
5. Pour the garlic and ginger mixture over the lobster. Garnish with sliced green onions.

Rock Shrimp Tacos

Prep time: 15 minutes | Cook time: 15 minutes | Serves 4

- 1½ cups ripe avocado, diced
- ½ cup Mexican crema or crème fraîche
- ¼ cup fresh cilantro, chopped
- ½ jalapeño pepper, finely diced and seeded
- 1 tablespoon lime juice
- 1 teaspoon kosher salt
- ½ teaspoon ground black pepper
- ½ cup olive oil
- 1 tablespoon agave syrup or honey
- 3 tablespoons red wine vinegar
- ½ teaspoon kosher salt
- ½ teaspoon ground black pepper
- ½ head red cabbage, finely sliced
- 1 pound rock shrimp, peeled and deveined
- 2 garlic cloves, finely minced
- 1 teaspoon lime zest
- ¼ teaspoon red pepper flakes
- ¼ teaspoon cayenne pepper
- ¼ teaspoon ground cumin
- 2 tablespoons vegetable oil
- 8 corn tortillas
- ½ cup Cotija cheese
- Lime wedges

1. Prepare the avocado crema by combining the avocado, crema, ¼ cup cilantro, jalapeño pepper, and lime juice in a food processor. Purée until thoroughly combined. Season with salt and pepper and place in a bowl, cover with plastic wrap, and refrigerate for at least 1 hour.
2. Make the cabbage slaw: In a small bowl, whisk together the olive oil, agave syrup, and vinegar. Season with salt and pepper. Toss the cabbage with the vinegar mixture and refrigerate.
3. In a large bowl, place the rock shrimp, garlic, lime zest, red pepper flakes, cayenne pepper, and cumin. Allow to marinate for 10 minutes.
4. Heat a wok or large skillet over medium-high heat and add the vegetable oil. Once the oil is hot, add in the shrimp and stir-fry for 2–3 minutes until they are cooked through and pink. Remove and place on a platter.
5. Warm the tortillas in a cast-iron skillet. Divide the rock shrimp and cabbage among the tortillas. Top each taco with Cotija and crema and serve with lime wedges on the side.

Cucumber, Shiitake, Shrimp & Garlic Stir Fry

Prep time: 5 minutes | Cook time: 5 minutes | Serves 2

- 1/2-pound shrimp
  1 cup sliced peeled and sliced cucumber
- 1/2 cup sliced onions
- 1 cup sliced shiitake
- 1 tbsp. oil

1. Marinade shrimp in a Superfoods marinade. Stir fry drained shrimp in coconut oil for few minutes, add onions and shiitake and stir fry for 2 more minutes.
2. Add the rest of the marinade and cucumber and stir fry for a minute. Serve with brown rice or quinoa.

Chinese Prawns with Garlic

Prep time: 15 minutes | Cook time: 10 minutes | Serves 4

- 2 tablespoons of rapeseed oil
- 10 cloves of garlic (chopped)
- 1 teaspoon of chopped fresh ginger root
- 225 g can of chopped water chestnuts (drained)
- 1 cup of snow peas
- 1 cup of small white mushrooms
- 1 teaspoon of crushed red pepper flakes
- 1/2 teaspoon salt 1 teaspoon ground black pepper
- 450 g peeled and chopped jumbo prawns
- 1/2 cup of chicken broth
- 1 tablespoon rice vinegar
- 2 tablespoons of fish sauce
- 2 tablespoons of dry sherry
- 1 tablespoon of cornstarch
- 1 tablespoon of water

1. Heat the oil in a wok or in a large pan until it is very hot. Cook the garlic and ginger in the hot oil and stir until they are fragrant, about 30 seconds. Add the water chestnuts, sugar snap peas, mushrooms, red pepper flakes, salt, pepper and prawns to the pan.
2. Cook, stirring, until the prawns turn pink (2 to 3 minutes). Mix the chicken broth, rice vinegar, fish sauce, and dry sherry in a small bowl for 2 to 3 minutes. Pour into the shrimp mixture; boil and stir briefly to combine.
3. Mix the corn starch with water and add to the wok. Stir until the sauce thickens, about 2 minutes.

Ginger Garlic Shrimp

Prep time: 15 minutes | Cook time: 45 minutes | Serves 4

- 1 pound uncooked prawns (peeled and boned)
- 1 tablespoon of oriental sesame oil or vegetable oil
- 1 tablespoon of chopped garlic
- 1 tablespoon of chopped fresh ginger
- 1/4 teaspoon dried and crushed red pepper
- 3 tablespoons of soy sauce
- 2 teaspoons of cornstarch
- 1/2 cup low-salt canned chicken stock
- 1/4 cup rice vinegar
- 2 tablespoons of sugar
- 6 green onions, cut into pieces
- 1 cup of peas
- cooked rice

1. Combine the first 5 ingredients in a medium bowl. Add 1 tablespoon of soy sauce and toss to coat. Let the soy sauce stand for 15 minutes and place the cornstarch in a small bowl.
2. Gradually add the broth and stir until the cornstarch dissolves. Mix in the vinegar, sugar and 2 tablespoons of soy sauce and heat the wok or heavy large pan over high heat.
3. Add the shrimp mixture, green onions and snow peas and stir-fry until the shrimp are pink and almost cooked, about 3 minutes. Add corn starch mixture; stir until the sauce is thick, about 1 minute.
4. Serve with rice.

Garlic Butter Shrimp

Prep time: 10 minutes | Cook time: 10 minutes | Serves 4

- 1 pound large shrimp, peeled and deveined
- Salt and pepper to taste

- 2 tablespoons soy sauce
- 2 tablespoons oyster sauce
- 2 tablespoons butter
- 4 cloves garlic, minced
- 1 teaspoon ginger, minced
- 2 tablespoons chopped cilantro

1. Season shrimp with salt, pepper, soy sauce, and oyster sauce.
2. Heat butter in a pan over medium heat. Add minced garlic and ginger, sauté until fragrant.
3. Garnish with chopped cilantro before serving. Serve over rice or noodles.

Squid, Shrimp, Celery & Bitter Gourd Stir Fry

Prep time: 5 minutes | Cook time: 5 minutes | Serves 2

- 1/4 pound shrimp
- 1/4 pound squid 1 cup sliced celery
- 1/2 cup sliced bitter gourd
- 1 tbsp. coconut oil

1. Marinade shrimp and squid in a Superfoods marinade. Stir fry drained shrimp and squid in coconut oil for few minutes, add celery and biter gourd and stir fry for 2 more minutes.
2. Add the rest of the marinade and stir fry for a minute. Serve with brown rice or quinoa.

Smoky Tea-Steamed Oysters

Prep time: 10 minutes | Cook time: 10 minutes | Serves 4

- ¼ cup lapsang souchong tea leaves
- ¼ cup uncooked long-grain white rice
- 2 tablespoons chopped fresh ginger
- 4 garlic cloves, crushed and chopped
- 2 tablespoons brown sugar
- 12 to 14 oysters, scrubbed
- ½ cup water
- 2 tablespoons sriracha sauce
- 2 tablespoons oyster sauce

1. Combine the tea leaves, rice, ginger, garlic, and brown sugar on a square piece of aluminum foil and roll the edges up to form the foil into a shallow, ½-inch-deep saucer. The top should be open. Place the foil saucer in the bottom of the wok.
2. If you're cooking indoors, open any windows near the stove and turn your exhaust fan on high. If you don't have a way to exhaust air outside, do the next steps outdoors.
3. Turn the heat on high.
4. While the wok and smoking mixture are heating up, arrange the oysters on a rack so that the cup sides are on the bottom and the flat sides are on top. Place the rack in the wok, at least 2 inches above the foil.
5. Cover the wok with a domed lid. As the mixture heats, it will begin to smoke. First the smoke will be white, then light yellow, then darker yellow. When the smoke turns dark yellow (about 5 minutes), wait 4 minutes more. Then, without removing the wok cover, pour the water into the wok between the cover and the rim. Be careful to avoid direct contact with the steam.
6. Let the oysters steam for 3 or 4 minutes, or until the shells have opened up.
7. In a small bowl, combine the sriracha and oyster sauce to enjoy with your smoky steamed oysters.

Mixed Seafood, Spinach & Red Peppers Stir Fry

Prep time: 5 minutes | Cook time: 5 minutes | Serves 2

- 1/2 pound mixed seafood 1 cup spinach
- 1 cup sliced red peppers
- 1/2 cup chopped scallions
- 1 tsp. oil

1. Marinade seafood in a Superfoods marinade. Stir fry drained mixed seafood in coconut oil for few minutes, add red peppers and stir fry for 2 more minutes.
2. Add the rest of the marinade and spinach and stir fry for a minute. Serve with brown rice or quinoa.

Steamed Whole Fish with Ginger and Scallions

Prep time: 10 minutes | Cook time: 9 minutes | Serves 4

- 1 (1-pound) whole fresh fish (black bass, black cod, rock cod)
- 2 scallions, green and white parts, julienned on the diagonal
- 1 (1-inch) piece fresh ginger, julienned
- 2 tablespoons water, plus 1 cup
- 2 teaspoons light soy sauce
- Cooked rice or rice porridge, for serving

1. If the fish needs additional cleaning, use a paring knife to scale the fish, and use a knife or scissors to cut off any remnants of the gills. Clean the inside of the fish, drain, then pat dry with paper towels.
2. Arrange the fish in a pressure-safe bowl. Place the scallions and ginger on top, then add 2 tablespoons of water to the bowl.
3. Pour the remaining 1 cup of water into the Instant Pot and place a trivet inside. Place the bowl of fish on the trivet.
4. Lock the lid. Program to pressure cook for 9 minutes on high pressure.
5. If the fish weighs 1 to 1.1 pounds, quick release the pressure. If the fish weighs 1.1 to 1.25 pounds, let the pressure release naturally for 5 minutes, then quick release the remaining pressure.
6. Drizzle with soy sauce.
7. To serve, use one or two large serving spoons to scoop large pieces of the fish along the spine; check for small bones. Enjoy with rice or rice porridge.

Shrimp, Baby Corn & Lotus Root Stir Fry

Prep time: 5 minutes | Cook time: 5 minutes | Serves 2

- 1/2 pound shrimp 1/2 cup sliced baby corn
- 1 cup sliced lotus root
- 1/2 cup sliced onions
- 1 tbsp. coconut oil
- 1/2 cup sliced shiitake

1. Marinade shrimp in a Superfoods marinade. Stir fry drained shrimp in coconut oil for few minutes, add all veggies and stir fry for 2 more minutes.
2. Add the rest of the marinade and stir fry for a minute. Serve with brown rice or quinoa.

Sweet and Sour Fish

Prep time: 15 minutes | Cook time: 15 minutes | Serves 4

- 1 pound white fish fillets (such as tilapia or cod), cut into bite-sized pieces
- Salt and pepper to taste
- 1/2 cup cornstarch
- Vegetable oil for frying
- 1 bell pepper, diced
- 1/2 cup pineapple chunks
- 1/2 cup ketchup
- 1/4 cup rice vinegar
- 2 tablespoons soy sauce
- 1/4 cup brown sugar
- 1 tablespoon cornstarch mixed with 2 tablespoons water (optional for thickening)

1. Season fish with salt and pepper. Dredge in cornstarch and fry until golden brown and crispy.
2. In a pan, combine ketchup, rice vinegar, soy sauce, and brown sugar. Bring to a simmer.
3. Add bell pepper and pineapple to the sauce. If desired, add cornstarch slurry to thicken the sauce.
4. Toss the fried fish in the sweet and sour sauce. Serve over rice.

Sichuan Spicy Shrimp

Prep time: 15 minutes | Cook time: 10 minutes | Serves 4

- 1 pound large shrimp, peeled and deveined
- Salt and pepper to taste
- 2 tablespoons soy sauce
- 1 tablespoon black bean paste
- 1 tablespoon Shaoxing wine
- 1 tablespoon sugar
- 2 tablespoons vegetable oil
- 2 tablespoons Sichuan peppercorns, crushed
- 3 cloves garlic, minced
- 1 tablespoon ginger, minced
- 2 green onions, sliced

1. Season shrimp with salt, pepper, soy sauce, black bean paste, Shaoxing wine, and sugar.
2. Heat vegetable oil in a wok over high heat. Add crushed Sichuan peppercorns, minced garlic, and ginger. Stir-fry until fragrant.
3. Add the seasoned shrimp and cook until they turn pink and opaque.
4. Garnish with sliced green onions before serving. Serve over rice or noodles.

Salt and Pepper Squid

Prep time: 15 minutes | Cook time: 10 minutes | Serves 4

- 1 pound squid, cleaned and sliced into rings
- Salt and pepper to taste
- 1/2 cup cornstarch
- Vegetable oil for frying
- 2 tablespoons chopped cilantro
- 2 green chilies, sliced
- 1 tablespoon soy sauce
- 1 tablespoon black vinegar

1. Season squid with salt and pepper. Dredge in cornstarch and fry until golden brown and crispy.
2. In a separate pan, heat a bit of oil. Sauté chopped cilantro and green chilies until fragrant.
3. Toss the fried squid in the sautéed mixture. Drizzle with soy sauce and black vinegar. Serve immediately.

Curried Shrimp

Prep time: 6 minutes | Cook time: 10 minutes | Serves 4

- 1 pound large shrimp, shelled and deveined
- $1/2$ teaspoon kosher salt
- 3 tablespoons vegetable or peanut oil
- 1 teaspoon minced garlic
- $1^1/2$ tablespoons red curry paste
- 1 shallot, chopped
- 1 small green bell pepper, seeded and cut into bite-sized chunks
- $1/2$ teaspoon granulated sugar

1. Rinse the shrimp under cold running water and pat dry with paper towels. Place the shrimp in a bowl and toss with the salt.
2. Heat a wok or skillet over medium-high heat until it is nearly smoking. Add the oil. When the oil is hot, add the shrimp. Stir-fry briefly until they turn pink, about 1 minute.
3. Push the shrimp up the sides of the pan. Add the garlic and curry paste into the hot oil. Stir-fry for 30 seconds.
4. Add the shallot. Stir-fry, mixing the shallot in with the curry paste, for about 1 minute or until the shallot begins to soften.
5. Add the green bell pepper. Stir-fry briefly, then add the red bell pepper. Stir-fry for 2 minutes, or until the green bell pepper is tender but still crisp. Splash the peppers with the soy sauce while stir-frying.

Fried Oysters

Prep time: 15 minutes | Cook time: 10 minutes | Serves 4

- 1 1/2 cups all-purpose bleached flour with a high gluten content
- 280 ml of cold water
- 3/4 teaspoon salt
- 2 tablespoons of baking powder
- 2 tablespoons of peanut oil
- 5 cups of peanut oil
- 20 medium-sized fresh oysters, opened, removed from the shells, patted dry and dusted with flour

1. Mix all ingredients for the dough in a bowl and set aside. Heat the wok over high heat for 1 minute. Add the peanut oil and heat it to a temperature of 190 °C.
2. Spread the batter evenly on each oyster. When a little smoke picks up in the air, add the coated oysters to the hot oil. Fry 5 coated oysters in batches for 3 minutes or until the oysters are light brown in color.
3. Place the fried oysters in a colander that you place on a bowl to drain off excess oil.
4. Fry the last batch of oysters for about 4 minutes or until golden brown. Return the other fried oysters to the hot oil and fry for another 2 minutes until golden brown.
5. Always pay attention to the heating level of the oven during deep-frying. Reduce the heat if the oysters are getting too brown or increase the heat if the oysters cook slowly.

Fish with Oyster Sauce

Prep time: 9 minutes | Cook time: 25 minutes | Serves 4

- 1 pound white fish fillets, such as pollock or grouper
- $1/2$ teaspoon salt
- 1 egg white
- 1 tablespoon Chinese rice wine or dry sherry
- 3 teaspoons cornstarch, divided
- $1/3$ cup plus 4 teaspoons water, divided
- $4 1/2$ teaspoons oyster sauce
- 1 teaspoon dark soy sauce
- 3 tablespoons vegetable or peanut oil, divided
- 2 thin slices ginger
- 1 teaspoon minced ginger
- $1/2$ teaspoon minced garlic
- 1 scallion, finely chopped
- $1/4$ pound fresh mushrooms, thinly sliced
- $1/4$ teaspoon black pepper

1. Cut the fish fillets into $1 1/2''$ –$2''$ squares that are about $1/2''$ thick. Place the fish cubes in a large bowl and add the salt, egg white, rice wine or sherry, and 2 teaspoons cornstarch. Marinate the fish for 15 minutes.
2. In a small bowl, combine $1/3$ cup water, oyster sauce, and dark soy sauce. In a separate small bowl, dissolve 1 teaspoon cornstarch into 4 teaspoons water.
3. Heat a wok or skillet over medium-high heat until it is nearly smoking. Add 2 tablespoons oil. When the oil is hot, add the sliced ginger. Let brown for 2–3 minutes, then remove from the pan. Add the minced ginger, stir-fry for 10 seconds.
4. Add the fish. Let the fish sit in the pan briefly, then gently stir-fry the fish cubes for 1–2 minutes or until they turn white and are firm. Remove the fish and drain in a colander or on paper towels.
5. When the sauce has thickened, add the fish back into the pan. Stir-fry for 1 minute. Serve hot.

Shrimp & Bok Choy Stir Fry

Prep time: 5 minutes | Cook time: 5 minutes | Serves 2

- 1/2 pound shrimp
  2 cups sliced bok choy
- 1/2 cup sliced green onions
- 1/2 cup sliced Chinese celery
- 1 tsp. oil

1. Marinade shrimp in a Superfoods marinade. Stir fry drained shrimp in coconut oil for few minutes, add all vegetables and stir fry for 2 more minutes.
2. Add the rest of the marinade and stir fry for a minute. Serve with brown rice or quinoa.

Salmon Stuffed with Spinach and Shrimp

Prep time: 15 minutes | Cook time: 15 minutes | Serves 4

- 1 tablespoon extra-virgin olive oil
- 1 large onion, chopped
- 8 ounces portobello mushrooms, chopped
- 8 ounces fresh spinach, chopped
- sea salt
- ground black pepper
- 12 ounces raw shrimp, peeled, deveined, and chopped
- ⅓ cup mayonnaise (i like to use an avocado oil–based one)
- pinch ground nutmeg
- 1¼ pounds skin-on wild salmon fillets, cut into 4 pieces

1. Preheat the oven to 400°F. Line a rimmed baking sheet with parchment paper or aluminum foil.
2. In a large skillet, heat the oil over medium-high heat. Add the onion and mushrooms and cook until the vegetables are softened, about 3 minutes.
3. Add the spinach and stir until it wilts, about 2 minutes. Season with salt and pepper to taste.
4. Add the shrimp and stir until it turns opaque, about 2 minutes. Transfer the shrimp and vegetables to a bowl and set them aside to cool.
5. When the mixture is cooled, stir in the mayonnaise and nutmeg.
6. Cut a lengthwise slit into each fish fillet, but don't cut all the way through the fish. Sprinkle each piece with a little salt and pepper. Arrange the fish on the baking sheet.
7. Stuff as much of the filling as you can fit into each slit. Spoon the remaining filling on top of the salmon.
8. Bake until the salmon is cooked to your desired doneness, about 12 minutes, depending on how thick your fish is.
9. Remove the baking sheet from the oven and change the setting to broil. Broil until the stuffing starts to brown a bit, about 2 minutes. Enjoy!

Chapter 6

Vegetables

Celery-Tofu Pot Stickers

Prep time: 45 minutes | Cook time: 30 minutes | Serves 6

- 10½ ounces (300g) extra-firm tofu, drained
- 5 large celery stalks (10½ oz / 300g)
- 2 tablespoons sesame oil
- 1½ teaspoons sea salt
- ½ teaspoon granulated sugar
- Dumpling Wrappers or 1 pound (454g) store-bought dumpling wrappers
- Canola oil, for pan-frying
- Black vinegar or Dumpling Dipping Sauce, for serving

1. Squeeze out as much excess water as possible from the tofu. In a bowl, crumble the tofu with your hands into a texture similar to ground meat.
2. Remove the tough strings of the celery stalks by snapping the stalks in half and peeling off any remaining intact strings.
3. Set up a bowl of cold water. Bring a medium pot of water to a boil over high heat. Add the celery and boil it for 4 minutes, or until it is tender. Immediately transfer the celery to the cold water to cool. Drain the celery and squeeze out as much excess water as possible.
4. Finely chop the celery, and add it to the bowl of tofu along with the sesame oil, salt, and sugar, and stir well to combine.
5. Fill and fold the dumplings using the pleated crescent fold.
6. Working in batches, in a large nonstick skillet, heat 1 tablespoon of canola oil over medium heat. Place the dumplings in the pan, leaving ½ inch of space between them. Add ½ cup of water to the pan, then cover the pan and cook the dumplings for about 7 minutes, or until all the water evaporates. (If the water evaporates too quickly, add a little more.) When the bottoms of the dumplings turn crispy and golden yellow, remove them from the pan. Repeat this process to cook the remaining dumplings, using 1 tablespoon of the oil and ½ cup of water per batch.
7. Serve hot with vinegar or dumpling dipping sauce.

Spicy Hong Shao Tofu

Prep time: 10 minutes | Cook time: 20 minutes | Serves 4

- 1 pound extra-firm tofu, drained, and cut into 1-inch pieces
- ¼ cup cornstarch
- 1 tablespoon chinese five-spice powder
- 2 tablespoons light soy sauce
- ¼ cup cooking oil
- 1 tablespoon chopped fresh ginger
- 3 garlic cloves, crushed and chopped
- 1 teaspoon spicy sesame oil
- 2 tablespoons shaoxing cooking wine
- 2 tablespoons dark soy sauce
- 2 tablespoons oyster sauce
- 4 scallions, both white and green parts, cut into ¼-inch pieces
- rice or noodles, for serving

1. In a plastic bowl or zip-top bag, combine the tofu, cornstarch, five-spice powder, and light soy sauce and toss to coat evenly.
2. In the wok, heat the cooking oil over high heat until it shimmers.
3. Add the ginger, garlic, and tofu and shallow-fry it for 3 to 5 minutes, turning it over to lightly brown all sides.
4. Lower the heat to medium and add the sesame oil, wine, dark soy sauce, and oyster sauce, then let it simmer for 15 minutes, until the flavors meld. Serve over rice or noodles.

Sichuan Vegetables

Prep time: 2 hours | Cook time: 10 minutes | Serves 2

For The Sichuan Sauce:
- 1 tablespoon vegetable oil
- 1 tablespoon minced garlic
- 1 tablespoon minced fresh hot peppers (thai chilies or jalapeño)
- ½ tablespoon crushed dried chili pepper
- ½ tablespoon ground sichuan peppercorns
- ½ cup hoisin sauce
- 3 tablespoons thin soy sauce
- 2 tablespoon sweet soy sauce
- 1 tablespoon ground bean paste
- 2 tablespoons sugar
- 1 tablespoon sherry cooking wine
- 2 tablespoons shaoxing wine
- 1 tablespoon chinkiang vinegar
- 2 tablespoons white vinegar
- 1 tablespoon Chinese red vinegar
- 1 tablespoon sesame oil
- ¾ cup slurry

For The Vegetables:
- ¼ cup vegetable oil
- ¼ white onion, sliced
- 2 tablespoons minced garlic
- 2 tablespoons peeled and minced ginger
- ½ tablespoon dry chili peppers, slightly crushed, flash-fried
- ½ tablespoon sichuan peppercorns, slightly crushed
- ¼ cup snow peas, cleaned and trimmed
- ¼ cup string beans, cleaned and trimmed
- 1 cup water spinach, bottom stem trimmed and cut to 2-inch pieces
- ¼ cup deseeded thinly sliced red bell peppers
- 8 mushrooms (dried or fresh), sliced in half
- 1 cup sichuan sauce
- 2 tablespoons shaoxing wine
- 1 tablespoon MSG
- ¼ cup shelled peanuts, slightly crushed, flash-fried
- 1 scallion, sliced

For The Sichuan Sauce:
1. Place a sauce pot on medium heat and add the vegetable oil.
2. Add garlic, hot peppers, chilies, crushed dried chili pepper, and peppercorns, cooking through until soft, about 2 to 3 minutes.
3. Next, incorporate hoisin sauce, soy sauces, ground bean paste, sugar, and the sherry and Shaoxing wines. Bring the mixture to a boil.
4. Finally, add the vinegars and sesame oil. Bring back to a boil and add the slurry to thicken the sauce. Reserve.

For The Vegetables:
5. Heat a pan or wok on medium heat with the vegetable oil. Add the onion, garlic, and ginger, and cook through for 3 minutes.
6. Next, drop in the crushed dried chilies and peppercorns. Cook for 1 minute. Then add the vegetables and mushrooms. Stir well, cooking until soft, about 3 minutes.
7. Pour in the Sichuan sauce, Shaoxing wine, and MSG. Bring to a simmer.
8. Remove from pan and transfer to a platter. Top with peanuts and garnish with sliced scallion.

Hot and Sour Tiger Skin Peppers

Prep time: 10 minutes | Cook time: 5 minutes | Serves 4

- ¼ cup cooking oil
- 2 dozen shishito peppers (2 cups)
- 2 tablespoons chinese black vinegar
- 1 teaspoon spicy sesame oil
- 1 tablespoon soy sauce
- 2 tablespoons shaoxing rice wine
- 1 tablespoon sugar
- cooked rice, for serving

1. In a wok, heat the cooking oil over high heat until it begins to smoke.
2. Add the peppers and stir-fry for about 2 minutes, or until the pepper skins blister and char.
3. Add the vinegar, sesame oil, soy sauce, wine, and sugar. Stir for about 1 minute, or until the peppers are coated. Serve over rice.

Mixed Vegetables

Prep time: 10 minutes | Cook time: 8 minutes | Serves 2

- For Thickener (Slurry)
- 2 ½ teaspoons cornstarch
- 1 tablespoon water
- For Stir-Fry
- 1 tablespoon vegetable oil
- 1 clove garlic, minced
- 1 small red pepper, sliced
- 1 small carrot, sliced
- 4 mushrooms, sliced
- ½ cup bamboo shoots
- ½ cup water chestnuts
- 1 cup broccoli florets
- ½ cup vegetable stock
- Salt, to taste
- 2 teaspoons soy sauce

1. Combine the ingredients for the thickener and stir. Set aside.
2. Heat the oil in a wok over high heat. Add the garlic, and stir-fry until fragrant.
3. Add the red bell pepper, carrots, mushrooms, bamboo shoots, and water chestnuts. Stir-fry for 1 minute.
4. Add the bean sprouts and stir-fry for 2 minutes.
5. Add the salt, soy sauce, and adjust according to your taste.
6. Serve while hot.

Cauliflower & Green Onions Stir Fry

Prep time: 5 minutes | Cook time: 5 minutes | Serves 2

- 1 pound cauliflower 1 cup green onions
- 1/2 tsp. chili flakes
- 1/2 cup onions
- 1 lime slice
- 1 tbsp. coconut oil

1. Marinade cauliflower in a Superfoods marinade and chili flakes. Stir fry drained cauliflower in coconut oil for 4-5 more minutes.
2. Add the rest of the marinade, green onions and onions and stir fry for a minute. Decorate with lime slice and serve with brown rice or quinoa.

Eggplant, Mushrooms & Carrots Stir Fry

Prep time: 5 minutes | Cook time: 5 minutes | Serves 2

- 1/2 pound sliced eggplant 1 cup sliced mushrooms
- 1/4 cup basil leaves
- 1/2 cup sliced carrots and red peppers
- 1 tsp. oil

1. Marinade eggplant in a Superfoods marinade. Stir fry drained eggplant in coconut oil for few minutes, add all vegetables and stir fry for 2 more minutes.
2. Add the rest of the marinade and stir fry for a minute. Serve with brown rice or quinoa.

Eggplant with Garlic Sauce

Prep time: 10 minutes | Cook time: 5 minutes | Serves 4

- 3 tablespoons cooking oil
- 4 garlic cloves, crushed and chopped
- 1 tablespoon crushed and chopped peeled ginger
- 2 cups sliced (½-inch) eggplant
- 2 tablespoons shaoxing rice wine
- 2 tablespoons soy sauce
- ¼ cup chili garlic sauce, like lee kum kee brand
- 4 scallions, green and white parts, cut diagonally into ¼-inch pieces
- cooked rice or noodles, for serving

1. In a wok, heat the cooking oil over high heat until it begins to smoke.
2. Add the garlic, ginger, and eggplant. Stir-fry for 3 minutes, or until the eggplant has lightly browned.
3. Add the wine and soy sauce. Stir-fry for 1 minute.

4. Add the chili garlic sauce and stir for about 1 minute, or until the eggplant is coated.
5. Add the scallions and toss. Serve over rice or noodles.

Double Nutty Fiddlehead Greens with Sesame Seeds

Prep time: 5 minutes | Cook time: 10 minutes | Serves 2

- 1 pound fiddlehead greens, fresh or frozen
- 2 tablespoons olive oil
- 2 teaspoons minced ginger
- 1 teaspoon garlic salt
- 2 teaspoons sesame oil
- 2 tablespoons toasted sesame seeds

1. If using freshly picked fiddleheads, wash to remove any dirt and drain thoroughly.
2. Heat a wok or skillet over medium-high heat until it is nearly smoking. Add the olive oil. When the oil is hot, add the ginger and stir-fry for 10 seconds. Add the greens. Stir-fry for 1 minute, then stir in the salt.
3. Stir-fry for 1–2 more minutes, until the greens are tender but still firm. Remove from the heat and stir in the sesame oil. Garnish with sesame seeds.

Sesame Pepper Stir-Fry

Prep time: 20 minutes | Cook time: 15 minutes | Serves 4

- 1 small head of cabbage (thinly sliced)
- 2 red peppers (thinly sliced)
- 1 onion, sliced (optional)
- 8 cloves of garlic (finely diced)
- 4 teaspoons of grated fresh ginger
- 1/2 cup sesame oil, divided
- 450 gr. beef fillet (thinly sliced)
- 1/4 cup soy sauce
- 2 teaspoons of white sugar
- 1 teaspoon of ground black pepper
- 1 cup of water
- 4 teaspoons of cornstarch

1. Mix the cabbage and red bell pepper in a bowl. Mix the onion, garlic and ginger in a separate bowl. Heat a wok or large pan over medium-high heat. Add 1/4 cup of sesame oil.
2. Cook the beef and onion mixture in the hot oil and stir until the beef is browned on both sides for 3 to 4 minutes. Add the herb mixture to the beef mixture; Cook, stirring quickly, until the cabbage wilts, the onion begins to brown and the beef is completely cooked, about 5 minutes.
3. Stir 1/4 cup of sesame oil, soy sauce, sugar and black pepper into the beef and herb mixture; swivel to pull over. Mix the water and cornstarch in a bowl until the cornstarch is dissolved; add to the beef and cabbage mixture.
4. Cook and stir until the sauce reduces and thickens, about 5 minutes.

Broccoli and Tofu Stir Fry

Prep time: 5 minutes | Cook time: 25 minutes | Serves 4

- 1 tbsp peanut oil
- 4 cloves of chopped garlic
- 1 red pepper, deseeded and cut into strips
- 2 crowns of broccoli, cut into florets
- 1/3 cup chicken broth
- 3 tbsp soy sauce
- 1 tbsp dry sherry
- 2 tbsp corn starch
- 225 g. extra diced firm tofu
- 2 tbsp cashew pieces

1. Heat the peanut oil in a large pan or wok over high heat. Fry and stir the garlic for a few seconds until it begins to turn brown.
2. Cook and stir the broccoli and bell peppers for 5 minutes until the bell peppers turn soft and brown - Stir cornstarch, chicken broth, sherry and soy sauce together until the cornstarch dissolves.
3. Pour the sauce into the pan and bring to the boil. Cook the tofu for a minute, stirring until hot.
4. Place the cashew pieces on top and serve.

Chinese Cabbage Leaves

Prep time: 10 minutes | Cook time: 5 minutes | Serves 6

- 2 tablespoons of asian (roasted) sesame oil, 1 bunch of cabbage leaves, thinly sliced
- 3 tablespoons of gomasio
- 1 tablespoon mirin (japanese sweet wine)
- 2 cloves of garlic, minced or more to taste
- Salt to taste (optional)

1. Heat the sesame oil in a large pan or wok until it sizzles; Add cabbage leaves, gomasio and mirin. Stir the garlic into the kale mixture and cook until the garlic is fragrant (approx. 30 seconds); take off the stove.
2. Season with additional sea salt if desired.

Buddha's Delight

Prep time: 15 minutes | Cook time: 5 minutes | Serves 4

- ¼ cup cooking oil
- 4 garlic cloves, crushed and chopped
- 1 tablespoon crushed and chopped peeled ginger
- 4 ounces extra-firm tofu, drained and diced into ½-inch pieces
- 1 small carrot, julienned (½ cup)
- 8 sugar snap pea pods
- 1 small onion, cut into ½-inch dice
- 1 (14-ounce) can baby corn, drained and rinsed
- 1 cup chopped (½-inch) napa cabbage
- 1 (8-ounce) can straw mushrooms, drained and rinsed
- 1 (8-ounce) can bamboo shoots, drained and rinsed
- 1 (8-ounce) can sliced water chestnuts, drained and rinsed
- 2 tablespoons cornstarch
- 2 tablespoons shaoxing rice wine
- 2 tablespoons soy sauce
- 1 tablespoon toasted sesame oil
- 2 scallions, green and white parts, cut diagonally into ¼-inch pieces
- cooked rice or noodles, for serving

1. In a wok, heat the cooking oil over high heat until it begins to smoke.
2. Add the garlic, ginger, tofu, and carrot. Stir-fry for 2 minutes, or until the tofu begins to brown.
3. Add the pea pods and onion. Stir-fry for 1 minute, or until they are lightly coated with oil.
4. Add the corn, cabbage, mushrooms, bamboo shoots, and water chestnuts. Stir-fry for 1 minute, or until the ingredients are well combined.
5. Add the cornstarch, wine, soy sauce, and sesame oil. Stir for about 1 minute, or until the liquid is well distributed.
6. Add the scallions and toss. Serve over rice or noodles.

Sichuan Potatoes

Prep time: 10 minutes | Cook time: 5 minutes | Serves 4

- 3 tablespoons cooking oil
- 3 garlic cloves, crushed and chopped
- 1 large potato, julienned or shredded (2 cups)
- 1 teaspoon red pepper flakes
- 1 teaspoon five-spice powder
- 2 tablespoons chinese black vinegar
- 1 tablespoon soy sauce
- 2 tablespoons shaoxing rice wine
- 1 teaspoon spicy sesame oil
- 4 scallions, green and white parts, cut diagonally into ¼-inch pieces

1. In a wok, heat the cooking oil over high heat until it begins to smoke.
2. Add the garlic and potato. Stir-fry for 2 minutes, or until the potato begins to brown.
3. Add the red pepper flakes, five-spice powder, vinegar, soy sauce, wine, and sesame oil. Stir-fry for 1 minute, or until all of the ingredients are well combined.
4. Toss in the scallions. Serve immediately.

Steamed Tempeh with Chinese Broccoli In Hoisin Sauce

Prep time: 10 minutes | Cook time: 10 minutes | Serves 4

- 1 cup water
- 1 pound tempeh, cut into ½-inch cubes
- ¼ cup hoisin sauce
- 2 cups gai lan (chinese broccoli) cut into 2-inch pieces
- 1 tablespoon toasted sesame oil
- rice or noodles, for serving

1. In the wok, bring the water to a boil over high heat. Place a rack in the wok.
2. In a pie pan or shallow dish, toss the tempeh and hoisin sauce together. Place the dish on the rack.
3. Cover and steam for 8 minutes.
4. Add the gai lan to the pan and mix with the tempeh; cover and steam for another 2 minutes, until tender-crisp.
5. Drizzle in the sesame oil, toss, and serve over rice or noodles.

Tofu with Cashew Nuts Stir-Fry

Prep time: 10 minutes | Cook time: 10 minutes | Serves 4

- 1/2 (340 g) package of extra firm tofu (sliced)
- 2 tablespoons of whiskey
- 1 tablespoon of fish sauce
- 1 tablespoon light soy sauce
- 1 tablespoon of black soy sauce
- 1 tablespoon of oyster sauce
- 2 tablespoons of vegetable oil or to taste
- 1 cup of unsalted raw cashew nuts
- 5 cloves of garlic, chopped
- 1 onion, cut into julienne
- 3 tablespoons of palm sugar
- 2 fresh red chili peppers (sliced)
- 3 tablespoons of water
- 4 green onions (sliced)

1. Mix tofu, whiskey, fish sauce, light soy sauce, black soy sauce and oyster sauce in a bowl and marinate for 10 minutes. In the meantime, heat the oil in a wok over medium heat and let the cashews brown for 3 to 5 minutes.
2. Put cashew nuts in a bowl and pour out the oil. Put the garlic in the wok and stir-fry for 1 minute. Stir in tofu and onion and stir-fry for 1 minute.
3. Add the palm sugar and chili peppers. Fry for another 2 minutes. Add water and stir until everything is well mixed.
4. Take off the stove. Scatter cashew nuts and spring onions over the top.

Chinese Broccoli in Oyster Sauce

Prep time: 5 minutes | Cook time: 10 minutes | Serves 4

- 1 teaspoon sea salt
- 2 tablespoons canola oil, divided
- 1 pound (454g) baby Chinese broccoli
- 3 tablespoons vegetarian oyster sauce
- 3 tablespoons water
- 1 teaspoon Chinese light soy sauce
- 1 teaspoon granulated sugar
- ¼ teaspoon sesame oil
- ⅛ teaspoon ground white pepper
- 3 garlic cloves, roughly chopped

1. Bring a large pot of water to a boil over high heat. Add the salt, 1 tablespoon of the canola oil, and the Chinese broccoli. Cook the broccoli for 2 minutes, then immediately drain it in a large colander.
2. In a small bowl, mix the oyster sauce, water, soy sauce, sugar, sesame oil, and white pepper. Set the mixture aside.
3. In a wok or skillet, heat the remaining 1 tablespoon of canola oil over medium heat until hot. Add the garlic and stir for about 1 minute, or until it is golden and crispy. Transfer the garlic immediately to a small bowl, leaving the oil in the pan.
4. Add the sauce mixture to the pan and cook, stirring constantly, for 1 minute to thicken the sauce. Remove it from the heat.
5. Arrange the stalks, all in the same direction, on a plate and pour the sauce over them. Sprinkle the garlic on top.

Tomato and Egg Stir-Fry

Prep time: 5 minutes | Cook time: 5 minutes | Serves 4

- 4 tablespoons cooking oil, divided
- 4 scallions, green and white parts, cut diagonally into ¼-inch pieces, divided
- ¼ teaspoon salt
- ¼ teaspoon freshly ground black pepper
- 6 large eggs, scrambled
- 2 tablespoons shaoxing rice wine
- 1 teaspoon sesame oil
- 4 garlic cloves, crushed and chopped
- 1 tablespoon crushed and chopped peeled ginger
- 4 medium tomatoes, coarsely chopped
- 1 tablespoon cornstarch
- ¼ cup ketchup
- cooked rice or noodles, for serving

1. In a wok, heat 2 tablespoons of cooking oil over high heat until it begins to smoke.
2. Add half of the chopped scallions and the salt, pepper, eggs, wine, and sesame oil. Stir-fry for about 2 minutes, or until the eggs are set but moist on top. Transfer the eggs to a plate.
3. Pour in the remaining 2 tablespoons of cooking oil and heat it until it begins to smoke.
4. Add the garlic, ginger, and tomatoes. Stir-fry for 2 minutes, or until the garlic and ginger are fragrant and the tomatoes begin to brown.
5. Add the cornstarch and ketchup. Stir for about 1 minute to combine.
6. Add the remaining scallions and toss. Serve over rice or noodles.

Tofu Puffs

Prep time: 5 minutes | Cook time: 30 minutes | Serves 12

- ⅔ block extra-firm Tofu from Scratch or 1 (16oz / 454g) package store-bought extra-firm tofu
- 1 teaspoon sea salt
- 1 cup water
- Canola oil, for deep-frying

1. Cut the tofu into 1- to 1½-inch cubes.
2. In a small bowl, dissolve the salt in the water. Dip the tofu in the salt water, then pat it dry.
3. In a deep pot, heat at least 3 inches of oil over medium-low heat. When the surface of the oil begins moving slowly (250° to 280°F), working in batches, carefully place the tofu cubes into the oil, not overcrowding the pot. Fry for 8 to 10 minutes, until they float. Be patient with frying at low temperatures; if the heat is too high, it will overcook and harden the tofu's surface.
4. Increase the heat to medium-high. Continue frying the tofu for 2 to 3 minutes, until the surface turns a light golden color but is still soft. Remove the tofu using a spider strainer or a slotted spoon.
5. Freeze the tofu puffs in an airtight container or zip-top bag for up to 1 month.

Kale, Carrot & Green Peas Stir Fry

Prep time: 5 minutes | Cook time: 5 minutes | Serves 2

- 1/2 pound green peas 2 cups kale
- 1/2 cup sliced carrots
- 1/2 cup onion
- 1 tbsp. coconut oil

1. Marinade green peas in a Superfoods marinade. Stir fry drained green peas and kale in coconut oil for few minutes, add all vegetables and stir fry for 2 more minutes.
2. Add the rest of the marinade and stir fry for a minute. Serve with brown rice or quinoa.

Baby Bok Choy Stir-Fry

Prep time: 15 minutes | Cook time: 15 minutes | Serves 4

- 600 g baby bok choy
- 2 tablespoons of peanut oil
- 1 piece of fresh ginger, chopped (about 1 teaspoon)
- 2 spring onions (white and green parts), thinly sliced
- 4 cloves of garlic, thinly sliced
- 1 teaspoon of coarse sea or kosher salt
- 1 teaspoon of sugar
- 1/8 teaspoon of ground white pepper

1. Cut a piece off the end of each bok choy head. Cut the bok choy crosswise into slices. Wash the bok choy with cold water in several passes and dry in a colander or salad spinner until dry to the touch.
2. Heat the oil in a wok or in a large pan over moderate heat until it is hot, but not smoking. Add ginger, spring onions and garlic and stir-fry until flavored, about 15 seconds.
3. Add bok choy, salt, sugar and pepper and stir-fry for 1 minute. Add 1 tablespoon of water, cover and cook, covered, for about 30 seconds until they are wilted.
4. Uncover, stir-fry for 5 seconds, then cover again, turn off the flame and let it simmer in the residual heat until just soft, about 30 seconds longer.

Eggplant Parmesan

Prep time: 7 minutes | Cook time: 10 minutes | Serves 4

- 1 large eggplant, cut into $1/2$ pieces
- 1 tablespoon Italian seasoning
- $1/2$ teaspoon black pepper
- 1 tablespoon kosher salt
- $1/2$ cup grated Parmesan cheese
- $3/4$ cup all-purpose flour
- 3 large eggs, beaten
- 1 cup Italian bread crumbs
- 4 tablespoons vegetable oil
- 2 cups Marinara Sauce
- 8 slices mozzarella cheese
- $1/4$ cup chopped fresh Italian parsley

1. Season the eggplant with Italian seasoning, pepper, and salt.
2. In a shallow dish, mix together the Parmesan cheese and flour. In a separate dish, place the beaten eggs. In a third dish place the Italian bread crumbs.
3. Working with 1 piece of eggplant at a time, dredge the eggplant into the flour mixture, then in the beaten eggs, and finally the bread crumbs. Use fingers to gently adhere the bread crumbs to the eggplant and place on a baking sheet. Repeat with the remaining eggplant slices.
4. Heat wok over medium heat and add 2 tablespoons vegetable oil. In batches, fry the eggplant, for 1–2 minutes on each side until golden. Transfer the fried eggplant to a plate and tent with aluminum foil. Repeat with the remaining eggplant, adding more oil as needed.
5. Preheat oven broiler. Place the eggplant in a baking dish. Cover the tops with the Marinara Sauce and place 1 slice cheese on top of each eggplant slice. Broil until the cheese has bubbled and browned. Top the eggplant with parsley.

Steamed Eggplant in Garlic-Sesame Sauce

Prep time: 30 minutes | Cook time: 15 minutes | Serves 4

- $1/4$ cup distilled white vinegar
- 1 medium globe eggplant (1$1/4$ lb / 567g) or 2 Italian eggplants
- 3 tablespoons Chinese sesame paste
- 3 tablespoons water
- 1$1/4$ teaspoons sea salt
- 6 garlic cloves, peeled
- 2 teaspoons sesame oil
- 2 tablespoons chopped fresh cilantro
- Flat-bottomed stainless steel or bamboo steamer with a large pot

1. Fill a large bowl halfway with water and add the white vinegar. Peel the eggplant, cut it into $1/2$-inch-thick slices, and immediately submerge the slices in the water to prevent browning.
2. Heat a pot of water with a steamer on top over high heat. When the pot is steaming, reduce the heat to medium and place the eggplant in the steamer. Shingle the eggplant slices into the steamer, overlapping them slightly to allow steam to come in between. Steam the eggplant for 10 minutes, or until tender. Remove the eggplant from the steamer and let it cool.
3. Meanwhile, in a small bowl, combine the sesame paste, water, and salt and stir into a smooth sauce. Using a small food processor or a mortar and pestle, thoroughly mash the garlic into a paste.
4. Squeeze any excess water out of the eggplant and use your hands to pull it into small, bite-size chunks. In a medium bowl, combine the eggplant, sesame sauce, mashed garlic, sesame oil, and cilantro and stir well.
5. Serve as an appetizer or side dish.

Fine Chinese Tofu

Prep time: 10 minutes | Cook time: 15 minutes | Serves 3 - 4

- 1/4 cup chicken broth
- 2 tablespoons of hot bean paste and 2 tablespoons of soy sauce
- 450 g normal or soft tofu, drained and cut into cubes
- 1 1/2 to 2 tablespoons of corn, peanut, or canola oil
- 225 g ground pork shoulder (preferably 75% lean)
- 2 teaspoon of finely chopped garlic
- 2 tablespoon finely chopped peeled fresh ginger
- 1 tablespoon of cornstarch dissolved in 2 tablespoons of water
- 1 1/2 teaspoons of japanese sesame oil
- 1/2 to 1 teaspoon of toasted sichuan peppercorn powder
- 3 tablespoons thinly sliced shallot

1. Mix the broth, bean paste, soy sauce and kosher salt. Put aside.
2. Put the tofu in a saucepan of boiling water and simmer on a low heat while the rest of the dish is fried while stirring.

Poach The Pork While Stirring:

1. Heat a wok or large, heavy pan over high heat and add 1 1/2 tablespoons of corn oil. Add the pork and stir-fry, breaking up any lumps and adding the remaining 1/2 tablespoon of corn oil, if the meat sticks, until it is no longer pink.
2. Add the garlic and ginger and stir-fry over a moderate heat until it is very fragrant, about 2 minutes.

Finished Cooking:

1. Stir the reserved sauce, then add to the pork and bring to a boil. Drain the tofu in a large sieve and add to the sauce, stirring gently, stir the corn starch mixture and fry while stirring.
2. Bring the cornstarch mixture to the boil, stirring gently, and cook for about 15 seconds until it is thick and shiny, then turn off the heat and sprinkle with sesame oil, Sichuan peppercorn powder to taste and 2 tablespoons of spring onions.
3. Stir once or twice, then serve sprinkled with the remaining tablespoons of spring onions.

Sichuan Five-Spice Crumbled Tofu and Vegetables

Prep time: 10 minutes | Cook time: 10 minutes | Serves 4

- 1 pound extra-firm tofu, drained and crumbled
- 1 tablespoon shaoxing cooking wine
- 1 tablespoon cornstarch
- 1 tablespoon chinese five-spice powder
- 1 teaspoon red pepper flakes
- 1 teaspoon spicy sesame oil
- ¼ teaspoon crushed sichuan peppercorns
- 3 tablespoons cooking oil
- 2 tablespoons hoisin sauce

1. In a bowl or zip-top bag, combine the tofu, wine, cornstarch, five-spice powder, red pepper flakes, sesame oil, and Sichuan peppercorns, and mix well.
2. In the wok, heat the cooking oil over high heat until it shimmers.
3. Add the tofu, ginger, and garlic and stir-fry for 2 minutes, until the tofu is lightly browned.
4. Add the Brussels sprouts and stir-fry for 2 minutes, until bright green.
5. Add the carrot and potato and stir-fry for 2 minutes, until softened.
6. Pour in the hoisin sauce, toss, and serve.

Chapter 7

Noodles and Rice

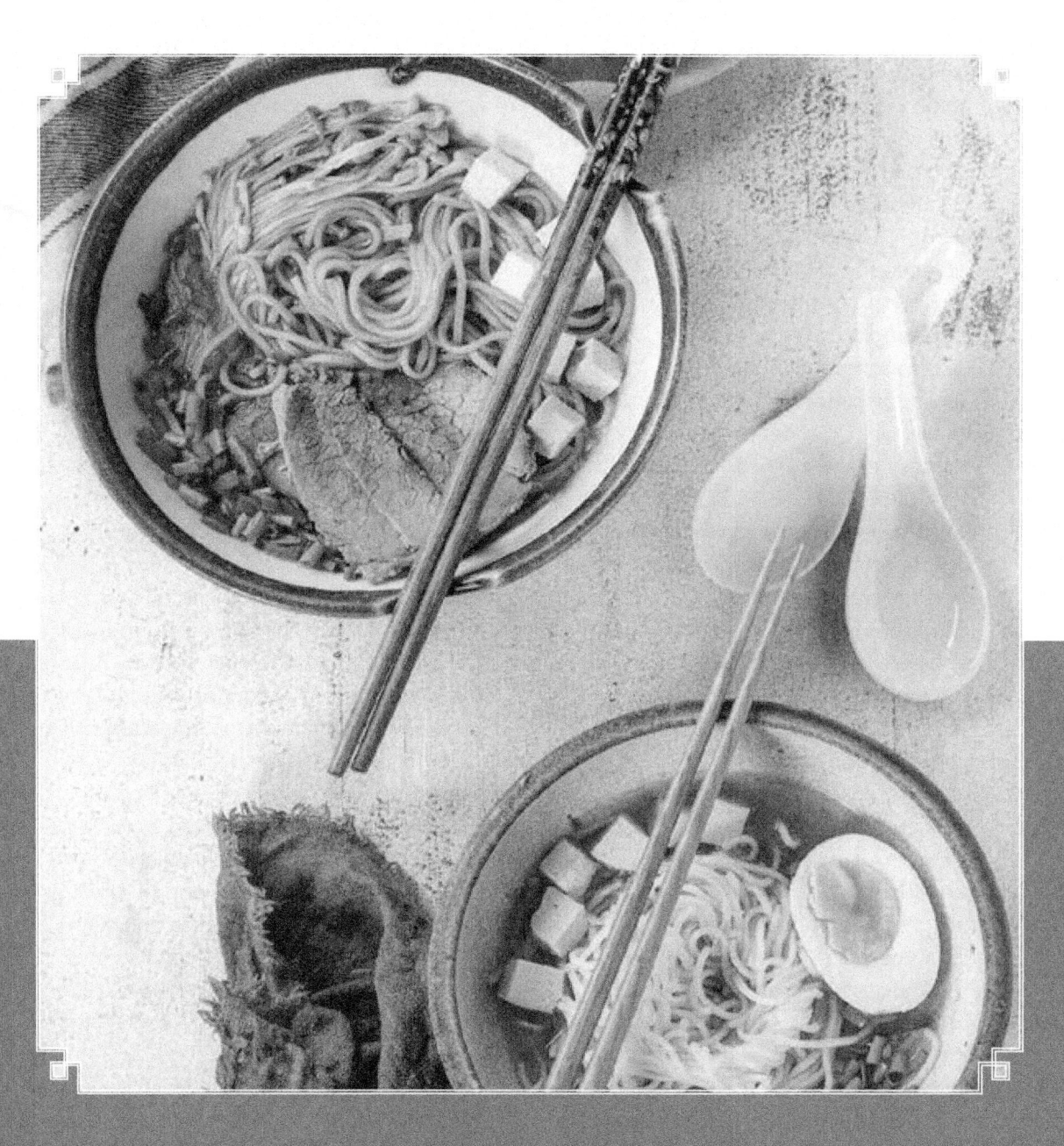

Beef Chow Fun

Prep time: 1 hour | Cook time: 5 minutes | Serves 2 to 3

- 8 ounces flank steak, cut across the grain in strips
- For The Marinade
- ¼ teaspoon baking soda
- 1 teaspoon cornstarch
- 1 teaspoon soy sauce
- 1 teaspoon oil
- For The Rest Of The Dish
- 3 tablespoons oil, divided
- 1 thumb ginger, cut into thin slices
- 4 scallions, halved lengthwise and cut into 3-inch pieces
- 1 12-ounce pack fresh flat rice noodles, pre-cut
- 2 tablespoons rice wine
- ½ teaspoon sesame oil
- 2 tablespoons dark soy sauce
- 2 tablespoons regular soy sauce
- ⅛ teaspoon sugar
- Salt and white pepper, to taste
- 4 ounces fresh mung bean sprouts

1. Mix the ingredients for the marinade together, and marinate the beef for 1 hour.
2. Heat the wok to smoking. Add 1 ½ teaspoons of oil, and sear the beef until browned. Remove the beef from wok and set it aside.
3. Add the rest of the oil and cook the ginger until fragrant.
4. Add the scallions and noodles, spreading them evenly inside the wok.
5. Stir-fry over high heat for about 15 seconds.
6. Add the wine, spooning it around the rim of the wok.
7. Add the sesame oil, soy sauces, sugar and white pepper. Scrape the bottom of the wok with a spatula, and lift the noodles upwards to mix.

Ants Climbing A Tree

Prep time: 15 minutes | Cook time: 5 minutes | Serves 4

4 ounces rice stick noodles
1 teaspoon sesame oil
2 tablespoons cooking oil, divided
1 teaspoon chopped fresh ginger, minced
1 teaspoon garlic, crushed and chopped
2 teaspoons doubanjiang (chinese chili bean paste)
4 ounces ground lean pork
¼ teaspoon freshly ground black pepper
1 teaspoon shaoxing cooking wine
1 teaspoon light soy sauce
1 teaspoon dark soy sauce
½ teaspoon sugar
1 cup chicken broth
sea salt
1 teaspoon finely chopped red bell pepper, for garnishing
1 scallion, finely chopped, for garnishing

1. In a large bowl, soak the rice noodles in warm water for 15 minutes, or until soft. Drain the noodles and toss with the sesame oil to keep separated. Discard the water.
2. In the wok, heat the cooking oil over high heat until it shimmers. Add the ginger and garlic, and stir-fry until fragrant, about 10 seconds. Add the doubanjiang and stir-fry for about 1 minute, until fiery and blended.
3. Add the ground pork and stir-fry until it separates into bits. Add the black pepper, wine, light and dark soy sauces, sugar, and broth, and bring to a simmer. Add the noodles and stir occasionally until most of the broth has evaporated. Season with salt.
4. Garnish with the bell pepper and scallion greens.

Hot and Sour Noodle Soup

Prep time: 15 minutes | Cook time: 20 minutes | Serves 4

- 8 ounces thin Chinese wheat noodles or rice vermicelli
- 6 cups vegetable or chicken broth
- 2 tablespoons soy sauce
- 2 tablespoons rice vinegar
- 1 tablespoon chili oil
- 1 tablespoon sesame oil
- 1 tablespoon sugar
- 1 cup shiitake mushrooms, sliced
- 1 cup tofu, diced
- 1/2 cup bamboo shoots, sliced
- 2 green onions, sliced
- 1 egg, beaten
- Fresh cilantro for garnish

1. Cook noodles according to package instructions. Drain and set aside.
2. In a pot, bring broth to a simmer. Add soy sauce, rice vinegar, chili oil, sesame oil, and sugar.
3. Add shiitake mushrooms, tofu, bamboo shoots, and sliced green onions. Simmer for 5-7 minutes.
4. Slowly pour the beaten egg into the simmering soup, stirring gently to create ribbons.
5. Divide cooked noodles among serving bowls and ladle the hot and sour soup over the noodles. Garnish with fresh cilantro before serving.

Ginger Peanut Noodles

Prep time: 15 minutes | Cook time: 10 minutes | Serves 6

- 3/4 cup smooth peanut butter
- 1 tablespoon honey
- 1/3 cup low-sodium soy sauce
- 1/4 cup rice wine vinegar
- 1 1/2 tablespoons toasted sesame oil
- 1 1/2 tablespoons sambal chili paste
- 2 tablespoons minced fresh ginger
- 1 tablespoon minced garlic
- 1 teaspoon lime zest
- 1/2 tablespoon fresh lime juice
- 1/4 cup water
- 1 pound Shanghai noodles
- 2 tablespoons vegetable oil
- 2 tablespoons minced shallots
- 1/2 teaspoon red pepper flakes
- 2 scallions, cut into 1 strips
- 1/4 cup crushed roasted peanuts
- 1 teaspoon toasted sesame seeds

1. In a blender, combine the peanut butter, honey, soy sauce, vinegar, sesame oil, sambal, ginger, garlic, lime zest, and lime juice. Blend until smooth. Add the water if the sauce is too thick. Set aside.
2. Fill a large pot with water and bring to a boil. Add the noodles and cook for 1–2 minutes. Drain the noodles in a colander and reserve 1/4 cup of the starchy water.
3. Ladle in 2–3 spoonfuls of the peanut sauce at a time until the noodles have been thoroughly coated. Add 1–2 tablespoons of the starchy water to loosen the sauce. Toss in the scallions and stir-fry until for an additional 30 seconds. Plate the noodles and top with the peanuts and sesame seeds.

Prawns and Fruity Fried Rice

Prep time: 20 minutes | Cook time: 1 hour | Serves 2

- 1 tablespoon of vegetable oil
- 2 eggs, beaten
- 225 g peeled and chopped medium-sized shrimp
- 1 piece of chopped fresh ginger root
- 2 sliced red onions
- 3 chopped green chili peppers
- 2/3 cup diced fresh pineapple
- 1/2 cup orange slices
- 6 chopped walnuts
- 2 cups of cold, cooked white rice
- 1 tablespoon of soy sauce
- 2 tablespoons of chopped fresh coriander
- Salt and pepper to taste

1. Heat 1 teaspoon of the vegetable oil in a wok over medium to high heat. Add the onions and cook until just cooked; put aside.
2. Turn up the heat on high and add another 1 teaspoon of oil to the wok. Stir in the prawns and cook for about 3 minutes until they turn pink and are no longer transparent in the middle; put aside; wipe out the wok and heat the remaining teaspoon of oil over high heat.
3. Stir in the ginger and cook quickly for a few seconds until the ginger starts to turn golden brown. Stir in the onion and chili peppers; let them cook for a minute or two, until the onions soften and turn brown around the edges.
4. Add pineapple and oranges and cook gently until pineapple is spicy; Stir in rice, walnuts and soy sauce. Stir for a few minutes until the rice is hot.
5. Fold in egg, prawns and coriander.
6. Season with salt and pepper and cook to warm up.

Vegan Drunken Noodles

Prep time: 15 minutes | Cook time: 25 minutes | Serves 2-4

Sauce:
- 5 tbsp (75 ml) sweet soy sauce
- 3 tbsp (45 ml) vegetarian oyster sauce
- 3 tbsp (45 ml) maggi sauce
- 2 tbsp (30 g) sugar
- 2 tsp (10 ml) sriracha sauce
- 2 tsp (6 g) minced garlic
- 6–8 thai basil leaves, chiffonade cut

Drunken Noodles:
- 3 tbsp (45 ml) canola or peanut oil
- 2– 3 cloves garlic, minced
- 1–2 serrano chilies, sliced thin
- 5 oz (145 g) extra-firm tofu, cut into ¾" (2-cm) large dice
- ½ medium white onion, sliced
- 3– 4 cups (675–910 g) fresh rice noodles, separated
- ½ cup (120 g) grape tomatoes, halved
- 1 cup (40 g) thai basil leaves, loosely packed

For the Sauce:
1. Combine the sauce ingredients in a small bowl and set it aside.

For the Drunken Noodles:
1. Heat the oil over medium-high heat in a medium-sized sauté pan. At the first wisps of white smoke, sauté the garlic until it is light brown. Stir in the chilies, diced tofu and onion, folding constantly until the tofu starts to brown, about 1 to 2 minutes.
2. Add the fresh rice noodles and sauté until the noodles are soft and slightly browned on the edges, about 2 minutes.
3. Add the sauce, tomatoes and basil. Toss them together to combine for about 3 to 5 minutes. Make sure the noodles completely absorb the sauce.

Cantonese-Style Beef Chow Fun

Prep time: 20 minutes | Cook time: 10 minutes | Serves 4

- 8 ounces fresh wide rice noodles
- 2 tablespoons vegetable oil
- 8 ounces flank steak, thinly sliced
- 1 tablespoon soy sauce
- 1 tablespoon oyster sauce
- 1 tablespoon Shaoxing wine
- 1 teaspoon sugar
- 2 cups bean sprouts
- 2 green onions, cut into 2-inch pieces
- 1 tablespoon soy sauce (for drizzling)

1. Separate the fresh rice noodles and set aside.
2. Heat vegetable oil in a wok or large pan over high heat. Add sliced flank steak and stir-fry until browned.
3. Add rice noodles to the wok and toss to combine with the beef.
4. In a small bowl, mix soy sauce, oyster sauce, Shaoxing wine, and sugar. Pour over the noodles and toss until well-coated.
5. Add bean sprouts and green onions, continue to toss until everything is heated through. Drizzle with a bit more soy sauce before serving.

Chicken Chow Mein

Prep time: 3½ hours + overnight | Cook time: 9 minutes | Serves 2

- 4 ounces sliced chicken breast, velveted
- ¼ cup mushroom water
- 1 cup + 3 tablespoons vegetable oil (additional oil required for your fry pot; see)
- ¼ cup salt
- ⅓ pound panfried or chow mein noodles
- 1 tablespoon minced ginger
- 1 tablespoon minced garlic
- 2 tablespoons small-diced white onion
- ¼ cup dried mushrooms, sliced (from mushroom water, see)
- ¼ cup snow peas, cleaned and trimmed
- ½ cup chicken stock
- 2 tablespoons oyster sauce
- 2 tablespoons soy sauce
- ¼ cup shaoxing wine
- 1 tablespoon MSG
- ¼ cup slurry
- 2 tablespoons sliced scallions
- ¼ cup bean sprouts, washed

1. First, prepare the velvet marinade, submerge your chicken, cover, and let it rest for three hours or overnight in the refrigerator. Separately, prepare your mushroom water and let it rest in the refrigerator overnight. (See for velveting and mushroom water ingredients and instructions.)
2. Fill your blanching pot with water three-quarters of the way and set to high, then add ½ cup of oil and the salt. When the pot comes to a rolling boil, drop your noodles into the pot, and cook for 1 to 2 minutes.
3. Remove from the pot, strain, and place on a plate. Do not shock. Pull the noodles slightly to form a rough pancake shape, about 1 inch thick.
4. Next, heat a sauté pan or wok on medium heat and add ½ cup of oil to pan. Add the noodle pancake, flip when it's golden brown, about 3 to 5 minutes, and brown other side. Transfer to a shallow bowl.
5. Next, add the oyster sauce, soy sauce, Shaoxing wine, mushroom water, and MSG. Thicken the sauce by adding the slurry.
6. Top the noodle pancake with vegetables, chicken, and sauce. Garnish the whole dish with scallions and bean sprouts.

Steamed White Rice

Prep time: 15 minutes | Cook time: 4 minutes | Serves 4

- 1½ cups white rice (your choice)
- 1½ cups water

1. In a medium bowl, rinse and drain the rice two times, then soak it in water for at least 10 minutes.
2. Drain the rice and pour it into the Instant Pot. Pour in the water.
3. Lock the lid. Program to pressure cook for 4 minutes on high pressure.
4. When the timer sounds, let the pressure release naturally for 10 minutes, then quick release any remaining pressure. Fluff the rice and serve.

Grapes and Rice Stir Fry

Prep time: 15 minutes | Cook time: 10 minutes | Serves 4

- 1 tbsp vegetable oil
- 1 cup of sliced red grapes
- 1 cup of diced cooked chicken
- 2 cups of cooked rice
- 1/4 cup chicken broth

1. Heat the vegetable oil in a large pan or wok over medium to high heat. Add the chicken and grapes.
2. Cook for about 3 minutes until the grapes are tender and the chicken is well heated.
3. Pour in the chicken broth and rice. Keep cooking

Tea-Smoked Beef and Vegetable Fried Rice

Prep time: 10 minutes | Cook time: 5 minutes | Serves 4

- 2 cups leftover lapsang souchong tea rice

- 1 tablespoon toasted sesame oil
- 1 tablespoon light soy sauce
- 2 tablespoons cooking oil
- 1 tablespoon chopped fresh ginger
- 2 garlic cloves, crushed and chopped
- 8 ounces ground beef
- 2 tablespoons shaoxing cooking wine
- 3 large eggs, beaten
- 1 medium onion, diced into ½-inch pieces
- 1 medium red bell pepper, diced into ½-inch pieces
- 4 scallions, both white and green parts, sliced into ¼-inch pieces

1. In a large bowl, combine the rice, sesame oil, and soy sauce.
2. In the wok, heat the cooking oil over high heat until it shimmers.
3. Add the ginger, garlic, ground beef, and wine and stir-fry for 2 minutes, until browned and fragrant.
4. Add the eggs and stir-fry for 2 minutes, until the eggs are firm.
5. Add the onion and bell pepper and stir-fry for 1 minute to mix well.
6. Add the rice and scallions and stir-fry for 1 minute to mix well. Serve immediately.

Ground Beef with Broccoli and Rice

Prep time: 7 minutes | Cook time: 42 minutes | Serves 4

- 2 teaspoons salt, divided
- 1/4 teaspoon black pepper
- 1 1/2 teaspoons cornstarch
- 3/4 pound ground beef
- 2 teaspoons plus 3 tablespoons vegetable or peanut oil, divided
- 1 teaspoon minced garlic
- 2 teaspoons minced ginger
- 2 cups chopped broccoli
- 1/2 cup water
- 1 cup cooked white rice
- 1 1/3 cup Basic Chinese Brown Sauce
- 1 teaspoon granulated sugar

1. In a bowl, mix 1 teaspoon salt, pepper, and cornstarch in with the ground beef. Let the ground beef stand for 20 minutes.
2. Heat wok or skillet over medium-high heat until it is nearly smoking. Add 2 teaspoons oil. When the oil is hot, add the ground beef. Stir-fry, stirring and tossing it in the pan until there is no trace of pink and the ground beef is nearly cooked through, about 8–10 minutes. Remove the ground beef and drain in a colander or on paper towels.
3. Clean out the wok or skillet and add 2 tablespoons oil. When the oil is hot, add the garlic and ginger and stir-fry for 10 seconds.
4. Add the broccoli and stir-fry for 2 minutes, sprinkling with 1 teaspoon salt. Add 1/2 cup water, cover, and cook the broccoli for 4–5 minutes, until it is tender but still crisp. Remove the broccoli and drain on a plate lined with paper towels.
5. Heat 1 tablespoon oil in the wok or skillet. When the oil is hot, add the rice. Stir-fry the rice in the oil for about 1 minute or until it begins to brown.
6. Add the ground beef and broccoli back into the pan. Add the brown sauce, stirring quickly to thicken. Stir in the sugar. Stir-fry for 1–2 more minutes. Serve hot.

Pineapple Fried Rice with Ham

Prep time: 15 minutes | Cook time: 10 minutes | Serves 4

- 3 tablespoons of soy sauce
- 1 tablespoon of sesame oil
- 1/2 teaspoon ground ginger
- 1/4 teaspoon white pepper
- 2 tablespoons of olive oil
- 1 onion, diced
- 2 cloves of garlic (chopped)
- 2 carrots (peeled and grated)
- 1/2 cup of frozen corn
- 1/2 cup frozen peas
- 2 cups of diced pineapple
- 1/2 cup diced ham
- 2 green onions (sliced)

1. Whisk soy sauce, sesame oil, ground ginger and white pepper in a bowl, set aside and heat the olive oil in a large pan or wok over medium to high heat.
2. Add onion and cook for 3 to 4 minutes, stirring frequently, until soft and translucent.
3. Add garlic and cook for another 30 seconds. Stir in the carrots, corn and peas and fry constantly until the vegetables are soft (3 to 4 minutes).
4. Stir in brown rice, pineapple, ham, green onions and soy sauce mixture for 3 to 4 minutes. Cook for approx. 2 minutes, stirring constantly, until heated through.
5. Serve immediately.

Tofu and Soba Noodles

Prep time: 7 minutes | Cook time: 45 minutes | Serves 4

- 1 cup Chili Ponzu Marinade
- 10 ounces firm tofu, cut into 1 cubes
- ½ cup Ponzu Sauce
- 1 tablespoon miso paste
- ½ tablespoon honey
- 1 teaspoon sesame oil
- 3 tablespoons canola oil, divided
- ¼ teaspoon cayenne pepper
- ½ cup blanched edamame beans
- ½ cup thinly sliced cucumbers
- ¼ cup diced red bell peppers
- 10 ounces cooked soba noodles, cooled
- 2 scallions, minced
- 1 teaspoon toasted sesame seeds

1. In a shallow dish, combine the marinade with tofu cubes. Cover and refrigerate for 20 minutes, flipping the cubes halfway through.
2. In a large bowl, whisk together Ponzu Sauce, miso paste, honey, sesame oil, 2 tablespoons canola oil, and cayenne pepper. Add in the edamame beans, cucumbers, bell peppers, and cooked soba noodles. Toss well to evenly coat the ingredients. Cover the bowl and refrigerate for 20 minutes.
3. Remove the tofu from the refrigerator and blot dry with paper towels. Heat the remaining 1 tablespoon oil in a wok over medium-high heat. Toss in the tofu and stir-fry for 1–2 minutes until the cubes become lightly golden.
4. Remove tofu from wok. Toss with the chilled soba, and then toss in the scallions. Transfer to plates and sprinkle with the sesame seeds.

Dan Dan Noodles

Prep time: 15 minutes | Cook time: 10 minutes | Serves 4

- 8 ounces Chinese wheat noodles or spaghetti
- 2 tablespoons sesame paste
- 2 tablespoons soy sauce
- 1 tablespoon rice vinegar
- 1 tablespoon sugar
- 1 teaspoon chili oil
- 2 tablespoons vegetable oil
- 3 cloves garlic, minced
- 1 tablespoon fresh ginger, minced
- 1/4 cup green onions, finely chopped
- 1/4 cup roasted peanuts, crushed

1. Cook noodles according to package instructions. Drain and set aside.
2. In a bowl, mix sesame paste, soy sauce, rice vinegar, sugar, and chili oil.
3. Heat vegetable oil in a pan over medium heat. Add minced garlic and ginger, stir-fry for 30 seconds.
4. Pour the sauce over the cooked noodles and toss to coat.
5. Serve the noodles topped with chopped green onions and crushed peanuts.

Chapter 8

Dumplings, Soups and Dim Sum Favorites

Egg Drop Soup

Prep time: 5 minutes | Cook time: 5 minutes | Serves 4

- 4 cups chicken or vegetable broth
- 2 eggs, beaten
- 1 tablespoon soy sauce
- 1 teaspoon sesame oil
- 2 green onions, sliced
- Salt and white pepper to taste

1. Bring broth to a simmer. Stir in soy sauce and sesame oil.
2. Slowly pour beaten eggs into the simmering soup, stirring gently to create ribbons.
3. Season with salt and white pepper.
4. Garnish with sliced green onions before serving.

Deep-Fried Salmon and Miso Wontons

Prep time: 40 minutes | Cook time: 15 minutes | Makes 40 dumplings

- 1 (8-ounce) skinless salmon fillet
- 1 tablespoon white or yellow miso
- 2 fresh garlic cloves, crushed and chopped
- 1 teaspoon toasted sesame oil
- 1 tablespoon soy sauce
- 1 (12-ounce) package square wonton wrappers
- 2 cups oil, for deep-frying

1. In a food processor, combine and pulse the salmon, miso, garlic, sesame oil, and soy sauce.
2. To make the wontons, place a wonton wrapper on a work surface so it looks like a baseball diamond with you sitting behind home plate.
3. Fill a small bowl with water. Using a clean fingertip, paint around the baselines with the water.
4. Place a teaspoon of the filling in the center, where the pitcher's mound would be.
5. Bring home plate up to second base, folding the wrapper into a triangle, thereby enclosing the filling. Seal the edges.
6. In the wok, heat the oil to 350°F, or until a wooden chopstick dipped into the oil causes bubbles.
7. Deep-fry the wontons until golden brown color develops on both sides, flipping as needed.
8. Serve with your favorite dipping sauce.

Wonton Soup

Prep time: 30 minutes | Cook time: 15 minutes | Serves 4

Wontons:
- 1/2 pound ground pork
- 1/2 cup shrimp, finely chopped
- 2 tablespoons soy sauce
- 1 tablespoon sesame oil
- 1 teaspoon ginger, minced
- 1 egg
- Wonton wrappers

Soup:
- 6 cups chicken broth
- 2 cups bok choy, chopped
- 2 green onions, sliced
- 1 teaspoon sesame oil

1. Mix pork, shrimp, soy sauce, sesame oil, ginger, and egg for wonton filling.
2. Place a spoonful of filling in each wonton wrapper. Seal and fold.
3. Bring chicken broth to a simmer. Add wontons and cook for 5 minutes.
4. Add bok choy and cook for an additional 2 minutes.
5. Garnish with green onions and a drizzle of sesame oil before serving.

Chinese Rice Cake Soup

**Prep time: 10 minutes | Cook time: 15 minutes |
Serves 8**

Meat:
- ½ pound lean pork, cut into strips
- 2 teaspoons shaoxing wine
- 1 tablespoon light soy sauce
- ½ teaspoon sesame oil
- ¼ teaspoon white pepper
- 2 teaspoons cornstarch
- 1 teaspoon water

Soup:
- 4 tablespoons vegetable oil
- 4 ginger slices, julienned
- 3 scallions, sliced
- 1 small carrot, sliced
- 1 ¼ pounds napa cabbage, cut into 1-inch pieces
- 4 cups chicken stock
- 4 cups water
- ½ teaspoon white pepper
- 1 teaspoon sesame oil
- 1 tablespoon light soy sauce
- 1 pound rice cakes, oval-shaped slices

1. Mix pork with soy sauce, sesame oil, water, cornstarch, white pepper, and wine in a bowl.
2. Cover the pork and marinate for 20 minutes.
3. Sauté pork with remaining oil in a Mandarin wok until brown.
4. Stir in ginger and rest of the ingredients, then sauté for 4 minutes.
5. Pour in water, stock, white pepper, soy sauce, and cook the soup for 10 minutes.
6. Add the rice cakes and cook for 1 minutes on medium heat.
7. Serve warm.

Cream Cheese Crab Wonton

**Prep time: 15 minutes | Cook time: 25 minutes |
Makes 24 pieces**

- 8 oz (227 g) lump crab meat or snow crab
- 16 oz (454 g) cream cheese, room temp
- 2 green onions (whites only), very finely chopped
- 2 tbsp (5 g) finely chopped tarragon
- salt and pepper
- 24 wonton skins (square)
- 1 egg, slightly beaten, for sealing
- 2 qt (1.9 l) vegetable oil for frying

1. Press out as much liquid as possible from any crab meat you are using. Any excess moisture will soak through the wonton skins. In a medium bowl combine the crab, cream cheese, green onion, tarragon, salt and pepper either with your hands or a mixer with a paddle attachment.
2. Take a wonton skin, place 1 teaspoon of filling in the center of each wrapper. with a finger dipped in egg, moisten the 2 adjacent sides; fold over the opposing corner to make a triangle.
3. You have some choices with shape. You can make a purse, tortellini or traditional triangle wontons.
4. Place the completed ones on a tray. Uncooked, rangoons can be wrapped and kept frozen for 1 to 2 weeks and dropped into the fryer frozen.
5. Heat oil in a 4- or 5-quart (3.8- or 4.7-L) Dutch oven or pot until the oil reaches 360°F (182°C). Fry in small batches until golden about 2 minutes on each side and drain on a wire rack over a cookie sheet. I like to serve these with sweet chili or plum sauce.

Bean Curd Rolls

Prep time: 145 minutes | Cook time: 35 minutes | Serves 4

- 8 medium dried shiitake mushrooms (¾ oz / 20g), soaked in cool water for 2 hours or up to overnight
- 4 tablespoons canola oil, divided
- 1 teaspoon minced fresh ginger
- 1½ cups (4oz / 120g) finely julienned carrot
- 1½ cups (7oz / 200g) finely julienned canned bamboo shoots
- 3½ tablespoons Chinese light soy sauce, divided
- 2 tablespoons Shaoxing wine
- ½ teaspoon sea salt
- ½ teaspoon granulated sugar, plus 1 tablespoon
- 1 tablespoon sesame oil
- 1½ tablespoons vegetarian oyster sauce
- 2 tofu skin (yuba) sheets
- 1 tablespoon cornstarch
- ½ teaspoon five-spice powder
- Flat-bottomed stainless steel or bamboo steamer, lined with cheesecloth, with a large pot

1. Drain the mushrooms, reserving 1½ cups of the soaking water. Discard the shiitake stems. Squeeze the caps to remove as much water as possible and thinly slice them.
2. In a wok or large skillet, heat 1 tablespoon of canola oil over medium-high heat. Add the ginger, shiitakes, and carrot and stir for 2 minutes. Add the bamboo shoot, 2 tablespoons of the soy sauce, the wine, salt, and ½ teaspoon of the sugar and stir for 2 minutes. Remove the pan from the heat, then stir in the sesame oil and let the vegetables cool.
3. In a large, deep plate or tray, mix the mushroom soaking water, oyster sauce, the remaining 1½ tablespoons of soy sauce, and the remaining 1 tablespoon of sugar. Stir to dissolve the sugar.
4. Dip 1 sheet of tofu skin in the liquid mixture to soften it for 2 minutes. Squeeze out the excess liquid and lay the tofu skin on a flat surface. Place half of the filling in a horizontal log in the center, near the bottom of the sheet. Fold the bottom of the tofu skin up around the filling as tightly as possible. Fold the extra tofu skin on the sides of the log in toward the middle. Roll the log forward until the tofu skin wraps the log. Repeat to make a second roll.
5. Place the rolls into a steamer lined with cheesecloth (or a dish inside the steamer). Heat the steamer over high heat until it comes to full steam. Reduce the heat to medium and steam for 10 minutes.
6. Meanwhile, transfer the leftover liquid to a small pot. Stir in the cornstarch and five-spice powder. Heat the mixture over high heat, stirring constantly, until it thickens.
7. In a large nonstick skillet, heat the remaining 3 tablespoons of canola oil over medium-high heat. Add the bean curd rolls and fry for 1 to 2 minutes on each side, until golden and crispy.
8. Cut the rolls into 1-inch-thick slices. Arrange the slices on a plate and pour the sauce over top. Serve hot.

Classic Egg Rolls

Prep time: 10 minutes | Cook time: 15 to 29 minutes | Serves 8 to 10

- For The Marinade
- 2 tablespoons soy sauce
- 2 tablespoons oyster sauce
- 1 teaspoon rice vinegar
- 3 cloves garlic, minced
- 2 teaspoons fresh ginger, minced
- ½ teaspoon brown sugar
- For The Egg Rolls
- 1 pound ground pork
- 1 tablespoon cornstarch
- 2 tablespoons vegetable oil
- 2 cups cabbage, shredded
- 1 medium carrot, peeled and shredded
- Salt and pepper
- 1 package egg roll wrappers
- Peanut oil for deep frying

1. Combine the ingredients for the marinade in a bowl, blending well.
2. Add the ground pork and cornstarch and combine. It's best to use your hands, clean or gloved, to do this.
3. Let the mixture marinade for about 5 minutes.
4. In a wok, heat the vegetable oil over medium heat. Stir-fry the pork until it is no longer pink.
5. Add the cabbage and carrots, and cook until heated through (about 2 minutes).
6. Season with salt and pepper as desired, and remove from the heat.
7. Place one wrapper at a time on a clean surface or tray, in a diamond shape.
8. Add about ¼ or ⅓ cup of the pork filling close to the tip of the diamond at the bottom, closest to you. Do not put too much filling or the wrapper will break while frying.
9. Fold the bottom tip of the wrapper over the filling. Roll tightly once.
10. Fold the left and right corners inward, and continue rolling up to the top corner.
11. Moisten the top corner with a little water or a paste of water and cornstarch to seal the roll.
12. Repeat until all the filling or wrappers are used up.
13. Prepare the peanut oil by heating it in a wok over medium-high heat. The oil is ready when wooden chopsticks immersed in the oil release tiny bubbles.
14. Working in batches, fry the rolls until they are golden brown. For more efficient heating and to get crisp rolls, do not overcrowd the rolls in the oil.
15. Use a spider strainer or tongs to lift the rolls out of the oil, and place them in a dish lined with paper towels.
16. Serve hot.

Crystal Shrimp Dumplings

Prep time: 40 minutes | Cook time: 8 minutes | Makes 16 dumplings

For The Wrappers:
- 4 ounces wheat starch
- ¾ ounce tapioca starch
- ¾ ounce potato starch
- 1 cup boiling water
- 1 ounce vegetable oil

For The Filling:
- ½ pound 16/20 shrimp, peeled, deveined, and coarsely chopped
- ⅛ cup minced bamboo shoots,
- ½ tablespoon salt
- 1 tablespoon MSG

Tapioca Batter:
- ¾ cup tapioca starch
- 1 cup cold water

Cooking: Ingredients:
- ½ tablespoon vegetable oil (plus ½ tablespoon for each round of dumplings)
- 4 dumplings
- 3 tablespoons tapioca batter
- 1 cup water
- ½ cup abalone sauce (preferably lee kum kee)

Making The Dough:
1. Prepare your mixer with paddle attachment and place on setting 2. Place the wheat starch, tapioca starch, and potato starch in mixer bowl.
2. Add the water slowly and mix until it's smooth and pliable. Add oil and knead well. Wrap in plastic wrap and rest for 30 minutes.

Making The Filling: and Tapioca Batter:
3. Mix shrimp with bamboo shoots, salt, and MSG. Cover and refrigerate for 1 hour.
4. Add the cold water to the starch and stir well until it has dissolved.

Assembling Dumplings:
5. Cut the ball of dough in half. Roll one half of the dough into a long log, approximately 1 foot long by ½ inch wide. Cut ¾-inch nuggets off the log. Press a nugget down with palm of your hand. Use a rolling pin to flatten into a thin circle.
6. Place a ½ tablespoon of filling into the circle and fold over. with practice, you can incorporate pleats into the fold. See instructions for pleated folding on –.

Cooking The Dumplings:
7. Heat an 11-inch nonstick pan on medium heat and ½ tablespoon vegetable oil. Add 4 dumplings close together in pan, then spoon 3 tablespoons of tapioca batter into the bottom of the pan.
8. Next, add 1 cup of water to pan, cover, and turn to high heat. When the water has almost evaporated from pan, remove the lid, and let the bottom crust crisp up.
9. Slide the whole crust onto a plate and serve. Repeat process as many times as needed.
10. Spoon a tablespoon of abalone sauce on each portion.

Pork and Shrimp Dumplings (Jiaozi)

Prep time: 30 minutes | Cook time: 10 minutes | Makes 30 dumplings

Dough:
- 2 cups all-purpose flour
- 1 cup water (approx.)

Filling:
- 1/2 pound ground pork
- 1/2 cup shrimp, finely chopped
- 2 cups napa cabbage, finely chopped
- 2 green onions, finely chopped
- 1 tablespoon soy sauce
- 1 tablespoon sesame oil
- 1 teaspoon ginger, grated
- Salt and pepper to taste

1. Mix flour and water to form a smooth dough. Rest for 30 minutes, covered.
2. Combine all filling ingredients in a bowl.
3. Roll the dough into a long log, then cut into small pieces. Roll each piece into a circle.
4. Place a spoonful of filling in the center of each wrapper. Fold and pleat to seal.
5. Steam dumplings for 8-10 minutes until cooked.

Cream Cheese Wontons

Prep time: 10 minutes | Cook time: 20 minutes | Serves 6

- 8 ounces cream cheese
- 2 teaspoons sugar
- ½ teaspoon salt
- 4 scallions, chopped
- 1 pack wonton wrappers
- vegetable oil, for frying

1. Mix cream cheese with sugar, salt, and scallions in a bowl.
2. Spread the egg roll wrappers on the working surface.
3. Divide the cream cheese filling at the center of each wrapper.
4. Transfer the golden egg rolls to a plate lined with a paper towel.
5. Serve warm.

White Bean and Kale Soup

Prep time: 5 minutes | Cook time: 20 minutes | Serves 4

- 1 tablespoon extra-virgin olive oil
- 1 small onion, chopped
- 1 small carrot, peeled and chopped
- 1 celery stalk, chopped
- sea salt
- ground black pepper
- 4 cups vegetable broth
- 1 (8-ounce) bunch lacinato (black) kale, thick center ribs removed and discarded, leaves chopped
- red pepper flakes
- juice of ½ lemon

1. In a large soup pot, heat the oil over medium heat. Add the onion, carrot, and celery. Season with salt and pepper. Cook, stirring, until the veggies soften a bit, about 5 minutes.
2. Add the garlic, rosemary, beans, and broth. Bring to a boil, then reduce the heat to a simmer.
3. Ladle about half of the contents of the pot into a blender and blend until smooth (see Tip 1). Stir this purée back into the pot.
4. Stir in the kale and red pepper flakes to taste, cover, and cook for 20 minutes.
5. Remove from the heat and stir in the lemon juice.
6. Season to taste with salt and pepper. Enjoy!

Chicken Mushrooms Dumplings

Prep time: 10 minutes | Cook time: 20 minutes | Serves 24

- 48 dumpling wrappers
- 2 tablespoons vegetable oil
- 1 small onion, finely chopped
- 4 ounces shiitake mushrooms, chopped
- 6 dried shiitake mushrooms, chopped
- 1 pound ground chicken
- 2 teaspoons sesame oil
- 3 tablespoons soy sauce
- 1 teaspoon sugar
- 2 tablespoons Shaoxing wine

1. Sauté onion with oil in a Mandarin wok until soft.
2. Stir in mushrooms, chicken, and rest of the ingredients.
3. Sauté for about 7 minutes until veggies are cooked and soft.
4. Allow the filling to cool and spread the dumpling wrappers on the working surface.
5. Divide the chicken filling at the center of each dumpling wrapper.
6. Wet the edges of the dumplings and bring all the edges of each dumpling together.
7. Pinch and seal the edges of the dumplings to seal the filling inside.
8. Boil water in a suitable pot with a steamer basket placed inside.
9. Add the dumplings to the steamer, cover and steam for 10 minutes.
10. Meanwhile, heat about 2 tablespoons oil in a skillet.
11. Sear the dumpling for 2 minutes until golden.
12. Serve warm.

Paomo Soup

Prep time: 10 minutes | Cook time: 30 minutes | Serves 4 to 6

- 2 tablespoons cooking oil
- 1 tablespoon chopped fresh ginger
- 3 garlic cloves, crushed and chopped
- 8 ounces ground lamb
- 1 tablespoon chinese five-spice powder
- 1 teaspoon spicy sesame oil
- 2 tablespoons shaoxing cooking wine
- 8 cups broth (chicken, beef, pork, or vegetable)
- 4 to 6 (6-inch) pita breads
- 4 scallions, both white and green parts, cut into ¼-inch pieces, for garnishing

1. In the wok, heat the cooking oil over high heat until it shimmers.
2. Add the ginger, garlic, lamb, five-spice powder, sesame oil, and wine and stir-fry for 2 minutes, until lightly browned and fragrant.
3. Add the broth and simmer for 20 minutes, until the flavors meld.
4. Tear a pita into bite-size pieces for each bowl. Ladle the soup over the bread.
5. Sprinkle the scallions on top and serve.

Shrimp Dumpling Soup

Prep time: 45 minutes | Cook time: 10 minutes | Makes 20 dumplings

Dough:
- 1 cup wheat starch
- 1/2 cup tapioca starch
- 1/4 cup cornstarch
- 1 cup boiling water
- 2 tablespoons vegetable oil

Filling:
- 1/2 pound shrimp, finely chopped
- 2 tablespoons bamboo shoots, finely chopped
- 2 tablespoons green onions, finely chopped
- 1 tablespoon soy sauce
- 1 tablespoon sesame oil
- 1 teaspoon sugar
- 1/2 teaspoon white pepper

1. Mix wheat starch, tapioca starch, and cornstarch in a bowl. Pour boiling water over and stir until a dough forms. Knead in vegetable oil.
2. Combine all filling ingredients in another bowl.
3. Roll dough into a log and cut into 20 equal pieces. Roll each piece into a circle.
4. Place a spoonful of shrimp filling in the center of each wrapper. Pleat and seal.
5. Steam dumplings for 8-10 minutes until cooked.

Red Miso Soup with Tofu

Prep time: 15 minutes | Cook time: 25 minutes | Serves 4

- 3–4 cups (710–946 ml) dashi stock
- ¼ cup (50 g) fresh shiitake mushrooms, sliced very thin
- ¼ cup (50g) dried wakame seaweed, rinsed and chopped
- ¼–½ cup (50–100 g) red miso
- 4 oz (100 g) block soft tofu in water, cut into small cubes
- 2–3 scallions, finely sliced on a bias

1. Heat the stock in a medium saucepan over medium heat until just under a simmer.
2. Add the mushrooms and seaweed and allow to cook for about 5 minutes or until the mushrooms have softened.
3. Add the tofu and scallions; allow to cook for about a minute. The scallions will perfume the soup and give it an earthy sweetness.

Mock Bird's Nest Soup

Prep time: 20 minutes | Cook time: 10 minutes | Serves 4 to 6

- 4 ounces long rice (one bundle)
- 8 cups broth (chicken, meat, or vegetable)
- 1 tablespoon dark soy sauce
- ½ ounce dried, sliced mushrooms
- 4 ounces ground pork
- 4 ounces chopped ham
- 1 (8-ounce) can water chestnuts, drained and chopped
- 2 large eggs, beaten

1. Cut the long rice into ½-inch pieces and soak in hot tap water for 30 minutes. Drain.
2. In the wok, bring the broth to a simmer and add the soy sauce and sliced mushrooms.
3. Stir in the pork, ham, water chestnuts, and drained long rice. Cook for 3 or 4 minutes, until the pork is browned.
4. Stir the broth gently in one direction while drizzling the beaten eggs into the wok and cook for about 1 minute, until strands and billows of poached egg form.

San Xian Wontons

Prep time: 10 minutes | Cook time: 20 minutes | Serves 12

- 8 ounces shrimp; peeled, deveined, and chopped
- 8 ounces ground pork
- 8 ounces ground chicken
- 1 tablespoon ginger, minced
- ¼ cup scallion, chopped
- 2 tablespoons vegetable oil
- 2 tablespoons light soy sauce
- 1 tablespoon oyster sauce
- ½ tablespoon sesame oil
- ½ teaspoon ground white pepper
- ½ cup water
- 2 packages wonton wrappers

1. Sauté scallions and ginger with oil in a Mandarin wok until soft.
2. Stir in pork, chicken, shrimp, and rest of the ingredients (except the wrappers).
3. Sauté for about 8 minutes, then remove the filling from the heat.
4. Allow the filling to cool and spread the egg roll wrappers on the working surface.
5. Divide the pork-shrimp filling at the center of each wrapper.
6. Wet the edges of the wrapper, fold the two sides then roll the wrappers into an egg roll.
7. Add oil to a deep wok to 325°F then deep fry the egg rolls until golden-brown.
8. Transfer the golden egg rolls to a plate lined with a paper towel.
9. Serve warm.

Chicken Stock with Ginger

Prep time: 10 minutes | Cook time: 65 minutes | Serves 12

- 5 pounds chicken parts
- 16 cups water, divided, plus more as needed
- 1 (2-inch) piece fresh ginger, thinly sliced
- 1 teaspoon salt

1. Place the chicken in the Instant Pot and pour in 4 cups of water. Select Sauté and bring the water to a boil. Parboil for 5 minutes, or until the water starts to foam. Select Cancel.
2. In a large colander in the sink, drain the chicken and rinse it to remove any impurities. Rinse and dry the liner before returning it to the base.
3. Return the chicken to the Instant Pot and pour in the remaining 12 cups of water, or as needed to reach the maximum fill line. Add the ginger and salt.
4. Lock the lid. Program to pressure cook using the Soup function for 60 minutes on high pressure.
5. When the timer sounds, let the pressure release naturally for 30 minutes, then quick release any remaining pressure.
6. Carefully remove the lid. Remove the chicken (reserve the meat for other uses) and strain the stock through a fine-mesh sieve into a large pot. Or, if using the stock later, transfer to Mason jars or freezer-safe containers and cool in an ice bath. Refrigerate for up to 1 week, or freeze for up to 2 months.

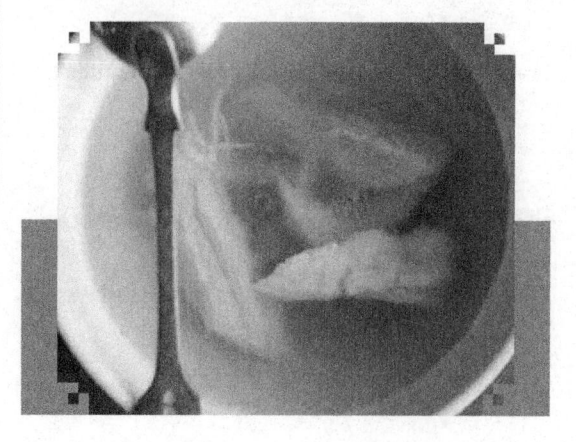

Chapter 9

Appetizers and Dessert

Purple Sweet Potato Sponge Cake

Prep time: 165 minutes | Cook time: 60 minutes | Serves 4

- 1 medium purple sweet potato (4oz / 113g)
- ⅔ cup warm water
- 2 tablespoons granulated sugar
- ½ teaspoon active dry yeast
- 1 cup all-purpose flour
- ½ cup jujubes, pitted and cut into small pieces
- Flat-bottomed stainless steel or bamboo steamer with a large pot

1. Place the sweet potato in a steamer and heat on high. When it comes to a full steam, reduce the heat to medium and steam for 30 minutes. Let the potato cool to room temperature, then peel and mash the flesh until smooth.
2. In a medium bowl, mix the water, sugar, and yeast; let it rest for 15 minutes.
3. Gradually add the flour to the yeast mixture, stirring to make a batter. Add the sweet potato and stir to combine. Stir in the jujubes.
4. Pour the batter into a deep 7- to 8-inch baking dish or cake pan lined with parchment paper and cover it with a large dish placed upside down (or anything that won't touch the batter) to prevent it from drying out. Let the batter rise on the counter for 2 to 3 hours, until it has doubled in size.
5. Place the baking dish in the steamer and heat on high heat. When it comes to a full steam, reduce the heat to medium and steam the cake for 20 minutes. Let the cake cool until you can touch it, then cut it into smaller pieces and serve immediately.

Red Bean Soup

Prep time: 5 minutes | Cook time: 1 hour | Serves 4

- 1 cup adzuki beans, soaked overnight
- 1/2 cup sugar
- Water
- Tapioca pearls (optional)
- Coconut milk for serving

1. Rinse adzuki beans and place them in a pot with enough water to cover.
2. Bring to a boil, then simmer for 1 hour or until the beans are tender.
3. Add sugar and continue to simmer until dissolved.
4. Optionally, cook tapioca pearls according to package instructions.
5. Serve the red bean soup warm, with a drizzle of coconut milk and tapioca pearls.

Chrysanthemum and Peach Tong Sui

Prep time: 5 minutes | Cook time: 15 minutes | Serves 4

- 3 cups water
- ¾ cup granulated sugar
- ¼ cup light brown sugar
- 1 tablespoon dried chrysanthemum buds
- 2 large yellow peaches, peeled, pitted, and sliced into 8 wedges each

1. In a wok over high heat, bring the water to a boil, then lower the heat to medium-low and add the granulated sugar, brown sugar, ginger, and chrysanthemum buds. Stir gently to dissolve the sugars. Add the peaches.
2. Simmer gently for 10 to 15 minutes, or until the peaches are tender. They may impart a beautiful rosy color to the soup. Discard the ginger and divide the soup and peaches into bowls and serve.

Cinnamon and Five-Spice Easy Donuts

Prep time: 15 minutes | Cook time: 25 minutes | Makes 16 small donuts

- 2 tsp (4 g) ground five-spice powder
- 2 tbsp (16 g) ground cinnamon
- ½ cup (95 g) sugar
- 2 cups (227 g) confectioners' sugar
- ¼ cup (60 ml) milk
- 1 tsp vanilla extract
- 1 (16-oz [454-g]) can large buttermilk biscuits
- 2 qt (1.8 l) vegetable oil, plus more as needed

1. In a large bowl, stir together the five-spice, ground cinnamon and sugar and set it aside. To make the glaze, whisk together the confectioners' sugar, milk and vanilla extract until the glaze is smooth and even.
2. Lay out the biscuits on a cutting board and cut them in half. Heat the oil to 365°F (185°C) in a 4-quart (3.8-L) Dutch oven. Fry the donuts in the oil for about 2 minutes on each side or until golden. Drain them on a wire rack over a sheet pan for about 2 minutes. Immediately dip one side in the glaze and top it with the spiced sugar.

Sticky Rice Pork Balls

Prep time: 10 minutes | Cook time: 35 minutes | Serves 4

- ½ cup sticky rice
- 1 egg
- 1 (1 inch) piece ginger root, minced
- 2 teaspoons soy sauce
- salt, to taste
- 4 ounces ground pork
- 2 tablespoons cornstarch
- 1 tablespoon pork stock

- ¼ cup of water
- 1 teaspoon dried goji berries

1. Soak the rice in water for 2 hours in a bowl.
2. Mix pork stock, pork, water, salt, soy sauce, ginger, cornstarch, and goji berries in a bowl.
3. Divide the mixture into meatballs.
4. Fill a cooking pot with water and set a steamer basket inside.
5. Boil the water and spread the balls in the basket.
6. Cover and steam these balls for 30 minutes.
7. Coat these steamed balls with rice.
8. Sear the steamed balls in a Mandarin wok greased with oil for 5 minutes.
9. Serve warm.

Potstickers

Prep time: 30 minutes |Cook time: 10 minutes|- Makes 24 potstickers

- 24 round dumpling wrappers
- 1/2 pound ground pork
- 1 cup napa cabbage, finely chopped
- 2 tablespoons soy sauce
- 1 tablespoon sesame oil
- 1 teaspoon ginger, minced
- Vegetable oil for frying
- Water for sealing

1. Mix pork, napa cabbage, soy sauce, sesame oil, and ginger.
2. Place a spoonful of the mixture in the center of each wrapper. Fold in half and pleat the edges to seal.
3. Heat vegetable oil in a pan. Add potstickers, flat side down, and fry until the bottoms are golden brown.
4. Add water to the pan, cover, and steam until the potstickers are cooked through.

Candyfloss Sweet Potato

Prep time: 5 minutes | Cook time: 25 minutes | Serves 4

- 4 medium sweet potatoes (1lb /454g)
- 3 tablespoons cornstarch
- 1 tablespoon canola oil, plus more for deep-frying
- ½ cup granulated sugar
- ¼ cup water
- 1 tablespoon distilled white vinegar

1. Peel and quarter the sweet potatoes lengthwise. Roll-cut them to form irregular bite-size pieces. Bring a medium pot of water to a boil over high heat. Drop the sweet potato into the water and cook them for 3 minutes. Drain the pieces of sweet potato in a colander.
2. In a large bowl, toss the pieces of sweet potato in the cornstarch.
3. In a deep pot, heat at least 3 inches of oil over medium heat. When a wooden chopstick lowered into the oil immediately sizzles (350°F), the oil is ready. Add the pieces of sweet potato and fry them for 5 minutes. Remove them with a spider strainer or slotted spoon.
4. In a wok or large skillet, heat the sugar, water, and 1 tablespoon of oil over medium heat. Continue stirring for 6 to 8 minutes, until the sugar has reduced to a golden syrup. Add the white vinegar, then add sweet potato. Flip everything for a few seconds to coat the sweet potato evenly. Transfer them to a plate immediately.
5. Eat this dish right away before the sugar coating hardens.

Mango Sticky Rice

Prep time: 15 minutes | Cook time: 15 minutes | Serves 4

- 1 cup glutinous rice, soaked for 1 hour
- 1 cup coconut milk
- 1/2 cup sugar
- 1/2 teaspoon salt
- 2 ripe mangoes, peeled and sliced
- Toasted sesame seeds for garnish

1. Steam glutinous rice until cooked.
2. In a saucepan, heat coconut milk, sugar, and salt until dissolved.
3. Pour the coconut milk mixture over the cooked rice and mix well.
4. Serve the sticky rice with sliced mangoes and garnish with toasted sesame seeds.

Black Sesame Soup

Prep time: 10 minutes | Cook time: 20 minutes | Serves 4

- 1/2 cup black sesame seeds
- 1/4 cup glutinous rice flour
- 1/2 cup sugar
- 4 cups water

1. Toast black sesame seeds in a dry pan until fragrant.
2. Grind the sesame seeds into a fine powder.
3. In a saucepan, mix sesame powder, glutinous rice flour, sugar, and water.
4. Bring to a boil, then simmer for 15-20 minutes until the soup thickens.
5. Serve the black sesame soup warm.

Calamari Fritti

Prep time: 5 minutes | Cook time: 50 minutes | Serves 4

- ¼ cup buttermilk
- 1 teaspoon garlic salt
- 1 teaspoon onion powder
- ¼ teaspoon cayenne powder
- 1 pound calamari, cleaned and cut into 1″ rings, tentacles left whole
- 2 cups vegetable oil
- 1 cup all-purpose flour
- ¼ cup yellow cornmeal
- 1 teaspoon kosher salt
- ½ teaspoon black pepper
- Lemon wedges

1. In a large bowl, mix the buttermilk, garlic salt, onion powder, and cayenne together. Add the cleaned calamari, ensuring it's well covered in the liquid. Cover the bowl with plastic wrap and place in the refrigerator for at least 45 minutes.
2. Place a large colander in the sink and pour the calamari with buttermilk mixture into it. Gently shake the colander to drain off the marinade. Use paper towels to blot off excess liquids.
3. Preheat oil in a wok to 375°F.
4. In a large zip-top bag, add the flour, cornmeal, salt, and pepper. Add the calamari and zip the bag closed. Shake well to evenly coat the calamari. Pour the contents of the bag into a large colander (or you can do this in batches) and sift the calamari to get rid of any extra flour.
5. In batches, carefully add the calamari into the hot oil and cook for about 3–4 minutes or until lightly golden and crispy.
6. Transfer the fried calamari to a paper-towel-lined plate. Repeat until all the calamari has been fried. Serve immediately with lemon wedges.

Chinese Seaweed Salad

Prep time: 10 minutes | Cook time: 15 minutes | Serves 12

- 12 ounces fresh kelp
- 4 garlic cloves, minced
- 3 thin ginger slices, minced
- 3 thai chilies, sliced
- 2 scallions, chopped
- 3 tablespoons vegetable oil
- 1 tablespoon sichuan peppercorns
- 1 ½ teaspoon sugar
- 2 teaspoons chinese black vinegar
- 2 ½ tablespoon light soy sauce
- 1 teaspoon oyster sauce
- ½ to 1 teaspoon sesame oil, to taste
- ¼ teaspoon salt
- ¼ teaspoon five-spice powder
- 1 tablespoon cilantro, chopped

1. Boil kelp in a pot filled with water for 5 minutes in a cooking pot.
2. Drain the kelp and rinse it under cold water.
3. Mix ginger, garlic, Thai chilies, and scallion in a bowl.
4. Sauté garlic mixture, and peppercorns with 3 tablespoons oil in a Mandarin wok for 10 minutes.
5. Pour this sauce over the boiled kelp leaves.
6. Serve warm.

Crab Rangoon

Prep time: 20 minutes | Cook time: 5 minutes | Makes 20 rangoons

- 8 ounces cream cheese, softened
- 1/2 cup crab meat, chopped
- 2 green onions, finely chopped
- 1 teaspoon soy sauce
- 1/2 teaspoon garlic powder
- 20 wonton wrappers
- Vegetable oil for frying
- Sweet and sour sauce for dipping

1. Mix cream cheese, crab meat, green onions, soy sauce, and garlic powder.
2. Place a spoonful of the mixture in the center of each wonton wrapper. Fold in half to form a triangle.
3. Seal the edges with water. Fry in vegetable oil until golden brown.
4. Serve with sweet and sour sauce for dipping.

Coconut Sticky Rice with Mango

Prep time: 15 minutes | Cook time: 25 minutes | Serves 4-6

- 3 cups (640 g) thai sweet rice
- 2 cups (480 ml) coconut milk
- 1–1½ cups (200–300 g) granulated sugar
- 1 tsp salt
- 4 manila mangoes, sliced into thin long pieces

1. Soak the sweet rice covered in water for at least 3 hours, preferably overnight.
2. Transfer the soaked rice into a bamboo basket. The rice should sit on the bottom of the basket. Add 4 cups (960 ml) of water into the steamer pot. Heat the water on high until it's boiling.
3. Insert the basket into the pot and cover

it for 10 minutes. Flip the rice once and let it steam for another 10 minutes.
4. Heat the coconut milk, sugar and salt in a small saucepan until simmering, then remove it from the heat. Reserve ¼ cup (60 ml) and fold the remaining coconut sauce into rice. Cover the rice for 30 minutes.
5. When ready to serve, drizzle the reserved coconut sauce over the rice, and serve with very ripe mangoes or any fruit in season.

Spring Rolls with Sweet Chili Dipping Sauce

Prep time: 30 minutes | Cook time: 10 minutes | Makes 15 rolls

- 15 spring roll wrappers
- 1 cup shredded cabbage
- 1 cup julienned carrots
- 1 cup bean sprouts
- 1 cup cooked and shredded chicken
- 2 tablespoons soy sauce
- 1 tablespoon sesame oil
- 1 teaspoon ginger, minced
- Vegetable oil for frying

1. Mix cabbage, carrots, bean sprouts, chicken, soy sauce, sesame oil, and ginger.
2. Heat vegetable oil in a pan and fry until golden brown. Serve with sweet chili dipping sauce.

Chicken Satay Skewers with Peanut Sauce

Prep time: 20 minutes | Cook time: 10 minutes | Serves 4

- 1 pound chicken breast, cut into strips
- 1 tablespoon soy sauce
- 1 tablespoon fish sauce
- 1 tablespoon curry powder
- 1 tablespoon brown sugar
- Bamboo skewers, soaked in water
- Peanut sauce for dipping

1. Mix soy sauce, fish sauce, curry powder, and brown sugar. Marinate chicken for at least 15 minutes.
2. Thread chicken strips onto skewers and grill or broil until cooked.
3. Serve with peanut sauce for dipping.

Scallion Pancakes

Prep time: 15 minutes | Cook time: 10 minutes | Makes 8 pancakes

- 2 cups all-purpose flour
- 1 cup boiling water
- Salt
- 1 cup scallions, finely chopped
- Vegetable oil for frying

1. Mix flour and boiling water to form a dough. Knead until smooth. Rest for 10 minutes.
2. Roll out the dough, sprinkle with salt, and spread scallions over the surface.
3. Roll up the dough and cut into 8 pieces. Flatten each piece into a pancake.
4. Fry in vegetable oil until both sides are golden brown.

Egg Tarts

Prep time: 20 minutes | Cook time: 20 minutes | Makes 12 tarts

- 1 package puff pastry, thawed
- 4 large eggs
- 1/2 cup sugar
- 1 cup evaporated milk
- 1/2 teaspoon vanilla extract

1. Preheat the oven to 375°F (190°C).
2. Roll out the puff pastry and cut into circles to fit tart molds.
3. Whisk eggs, sugar, evaporated milk, and vanilla extract in a bowl.
4. Pour the egg mixture into the tart shells.
5. Bake for 15-20 minutes or until the custard is set and the pastry is golden brown.

Almond Cookies

Prep time: 15 minutes | Cook time: 12 minutes | Makes 24 cookies

- 1 cup unsalted butter, softened
- 1 cup sugar
- 1 egg
- 1 teaspoon almond extract
- 2 1/2 cups all-purpose flour
- 1/2 teaspoon baking soda
- 1/2 cup almonds, finely chopped

1. Preheat the oven to 350°F (175°C).
2. Cream together butter and sugar until light and fluffy.
3. Beat in the egg and almond extract.
4. In a separate bowl, whisk together flour and baking soda. Gradually add to the butter mixture.
5. Fold in chopped almonds. Drop rounded tablespoons of dough onto baking sheets.
6. Bake for 10-12 minutes or until the edges are golden brown.

Appendix 1 Measurement Conversion Chart

Volume Equivalents (Dry)

US STANDARD	METRIC (APPROXIMATE)
1/8 teaspoon	0.5 mL
1/4 teaspoon	1 mL
1/2 teaspoon	2 mL
3/4 teaspoon	4 mL
1 teaspoon	5 mL
1 tablespoon	15 mL
1/4 cup	59 mL
1/2 cup	118 mL
3/4 cup	177 mL
1 cup	235 mL
2 cups	475 mL
3 cups	700 mL
4 cups	1 L

Volume Equivalents (Liquid)

US STANDARD	US STANDARD (OUNCES)	METRIC (APPROXIMATE)
2 tablespoons	1 fl.oz.	30 mL
1/4 cup	2 fl.oz.	60 mL
1/2 cup	4 fl.oz.	120 mL
1 cup	8 fl.oz.	240 mL
1 1/2 cup	12 fl.oz.	355 mL
2 cups or 1 pint	16 fl.oz.	475 mL
4 cups or 1 quart	32 fl.oz.	1 L
1 gallon	128 fl.oz.	4 L

Temperatures Equivalents

FAHRENHEIT(F)	CELSIUS(C) APPROXIMATE
225 °F	107 °C
250 °F	120 ° °C
275 °F	135 °C
300 °F	150 °C
325 °F	160 °C
350 °F	180 °C
375 °F	190 °C
400 °F	205 °C
425 °F	220 °C
450 °F	235 °C
475 °F	245 °C
500 °F	260 °C

Weight Equivalents

US STANDARD	METRIC (APPROXIMATE)
1 ounce	28 g
2 ounces	57 g
5 ounces	142 g
10 ounces	284 g
15 ounces	425 g
16 ounces (1 pound)	455 g
1.5 pounds	680 g
2 pounds	907 g

Appendix 2 The Dirty Dozen and Clean Fifteen

The Environmental Working Group (EWG) is a nonprofit, nonpartisan organization dedicated to protecting human health and the environment Its mission is to empower people to live healthier lives in a healthier environment. This organization publishes an annual list of the twelve kinds of produce, in sequence, that have the highest amount of pesticide residue-the Dirty Dozen-as well as a list of the fifteen kinds ofproduce that have the least amount of pesticide residue-the Clean Fifteen.

THE DIRTY DOZEN

The 2016 Dirty Dozen includes the following produce. These are considered among the year's most important produce to buy organic:

Strawberries	Spinach
Apples	Tomatoes
Nectarines	Bell peppers
Peaches	Cherry tomatoes
Celery	Cucumbers
Grapes	Kale/collard greens
Cherries	Hot peppers

The Dirty Dozen list contains two additional itemskale/collard greens and hot peppers-because they tend to contain trace levels of highly hazardous pesticides.

THE CLEAN FIFTEEN

The least critical to buy organically are the Clean Fifteen list. The following are on the 2016 list:

Avocados	Papayas
Corn	Kiw
Pineapples	Eggplant
Cabbage	Honeydew
Sweet peas	Grapefruit
Onions	Cantaloupe
Asparagus	Cauliflower
Mangos	

Some of the sweet corn sold in the United States are made from genetically engineered (GE) seedstock. Buy organic varieties of these crops to avoid GE produce.

Appendix 3 Index

Chloe Lee

Printed in Great Britain
by Amazon

38076815R00057